GREAT AMERICAN THINKERS

W. E. B. Du Bois

Co-Founder of the NAACP

Meghan M. Engsberg Cunningham

Cavendish
Square

New York

Published in 2017 by Cavendish Square Publishing, LLC
243 5th Avenue, Suite 136, New York, NY 10016

All websites were available and accurate when this book was sent to press.

Library of Congress Cataloging-in-Publication Data

Names: Engsberg Cunningham, Meghan M., author. Title: W.E.B. Du Bois :
Co-Founder of the NAACP / Meghan M. Engsberg Cunningham.
Description: New York : Cavendish Square Publishing, [2017] | Series: Great
American thinkers | Includes bibliographical references and index.
Identifiers: LCCN 2016003657 (print) | LCCN 2016004058 (ebook) |
ISBN 9781502619266 (library bound) | ISBN 9781502619273 (ebook)
Subjects: LCSH: Du Bois, W. E. B. (William Edward Burghardt), 1868-1963--Juvenile
literature. | African Americans--Biography--Juvenile
literature. | African American intellectuals--Biography--Juvenile literature.
| African American civil rights workers--Biography--Juvenile
literature.Classification: LCC E185.97.D73 C87 2016 (print) | LCC E185.97.D73 (ebook)
| DDC 323.092--dc23 LC record available at http://lccn.loc.gov/2016003657

Editorial Director: David McNamara
Editor: Elizabeth Schmermund
Copy Editor: Rebecca Rohan
Art Director: Jeffrey Talbot
Designer: Amy Greenan
Production Assistant: Karol Szymczuk
Photo Research: J8 Media

Printed in the United States of America

CONTENTS

INTRODUCTION ... 5
An Advocate for Social Justice

ONE ... 9
From the Civil War to Civil Rights

TWO ... 31
The Long Life of Du Bois

THREE ... 47
Du Bois and His Contemporaries

FOUR ... 61
Writing and Activism

FIVE ... 77
The Great Advocate

SIX ... 97
W. E. B. Du Bois and the NAACP Today

Chronology / 110

Glossary / 114

Sources / 117

Further Information / 120

Bibliography /122

Index / 124

About the Author / 128

INTRODUCTION

An Advocate for Social Justice

W hen William Edward Burghardt Du Bois was born in 1868, the Civil War had ended but the United States was still trying to become one country again. Slaves had been declared free with both the Emancipation Proclamation and the Thirteenth Amendment, but black citizens were far from having equal rights and equal access to opportunities. African-American culture at the turn of the century was made up of sons and daughters of former slaves who were trying to find their own identity within the greater American culture. Their citizenship was constantly challenged, most especially in the South immediately after **Reconstruction**.

Du Bois had a relatively happy childhood in his hometown of Great Barrington, Massachusetts. The town's black population was very small, so he went to a predominantly white school and

W. E. B. Du Bois (*left*) in one of his most famous portraits, circa 1911, shortly after the founding of the NAACP.

The Great Barrington Congregational Church (*left*) and its values shaped Great Barrington and the town Du Bois grew up in.

church. Du Bois graduated high school in 1884 with high honors—he was the first black graduate from Great Barrington High. After graduation, he went to work right away to support his mother and to save money for college. Although going to Harvard University was his dream, he first attended Fisk University. Eventually, however, he would become the first black man to earn a PhD from Harvard.

Du Bois's professional life can be categorized into three different areas: academia, writing, and activism. Before Du Bois had even graduated from Fisk, he spent his summers in poor, all-black communities teaching school and learning about black communities and culture in ways he couldn't in his own hometown. As a professor, he spent many years at Atlanta University (now Clark Atlanta

University). Atlanta was his home base when he wrote his most famous work, *The Souls of Black Folk*. That text articulated the psychological challenges of being black in the United States of America. With the publication of Du Bois's *The Souls of Black Folk,* his popularity grew, and he began to transition into activism. He traveled extensively to meetings hosted by the Niagara Movement, which he helped found, and gave speeches at numerous conferences. Eventually, he and a large group of influential people formed the National Association for the Advancement of Colored People (NAACP) in 1909. One of the few black founding members of the organization, his constant investment in fighting for the enfranchisement of all black citizens ensured the subsequent success of the NAACP.

The founding of the NAACP changed Du Bois's life. He left Atlanta University and took over public relations for the NAACP. He founded the *Crisis*, the periodical arm of the organization. He served as its editor-in-chief for many years. Today, both the NAACP and the *Crisis* continue to advocate for racial justice.

Toward the end of his life, Du Bois began to be more active in the **socialist** and **communist** parties of the United States. He traveled extensively and wrote prolifically. He also struggled with the lack of progress in guaranteeing African Americans their civil rights. Du Bois became increasingly disillusioned with racial discrimination and, toward the end of his life, he would emigrate from the United States. Even though he chose to become as citizen of Ghana, his contributions to American literature and racial equality forever changed the United States of America.

PROCLAMATION OF EMANCIPATION

1861 OF 1863

By the President of the United States of America.

Whereas, On the Twenty-Second day of September, in the year of our Lord one thousand eight hundred and sixty-two, a Proclamation was issued by the President of the United States, containing, among other things the following, to wit:

"That on the first day of January, in the year of our Lord one thousand eight hundred and sixty-three, all persons held as Slaves within any State or designated part of a State, the people whereof shall then be in rebellion against the United States, shall be then, thenceforth, and FOREVER FREE, and the EXECUTIVE GOVERNMENT OF THE UNITED STATES, including the military and naval authorities thereof, WILL RECOGNIZE AND MAINTAIN THE FREEDOM of such persons, and will do no act or acts to repress such persons, or any of them, in any efforts they may make for their actual freedom.

"That the Executive will, on the first day of January aforesaid, by proclamation, designate the States and parts of States, if any, in which the people thereof respectively shall then be in rebellion against the United States, and the fact that any State, or the people thereof shall on that day be in good faith represented in the Congress of the United States by members chosen thereto at elections wherein a majority of the qualified voters of such State shall have participated, shall, in the absence of strong countervailing testimony be deemed conclusive evidence that such State and the people thereof are not then in rebellion against the United States."

Now, therefore, I, ABRAHAM LINCOLN, President of the United States, by virtue of the power in me vested as Commander-in-Chief of the Army and Navy of the United States in time of actual armed Rebellion against the authority and government of the United States, and as a fit and necessary war measure for suppressing said Rebellion, do, on this first day of January, in the year of our Lord one thousand eight hundred and sixty-three, and in accordance with my purpose so to do, publicly proclaim for the full period of one hundred days from the day of the first above-mentioned order, and designate, as the States and parts of States wherein the people thereof respectively are this day in rebellion against the United States, the following, to wit: ARKANSAS, TEXAS, LOUISIANA (except the Parishes of St. Bernard, Plaquemines, Jefferson, St. John, St. Charles, St. James, Ascension, Assumption, Terre Bonne, La Fourche, St. Mary, St. Martin, and Orleans, including the City of Orleans), MISSISSIPPI, ALABAMA, FLORIDA, GEORGIA, SOUTH CAROLINA, NORTH CAROLINA, and VIRGINIA (except the forty-eight counties designated as West Virginia, and also the counties of Berkeley, Accomac, Northampton, Elizabeth City, York, Princess Ann, and Norfolk, including the cities of Norfolk and Portsmouth), and which excepted parts are for the present left precisely as if this Proclamation were not issued.

And by virtue of the power and for the purpose aforesaid, I do order and declare that ALL PERSONS HELD AS SLAVES within said designated States and parts of States ARE, AND HENCEFORWARD SHALL BE FREE! and that the Executive Government of the United States, including the Military and Naval Authorities thereof, will RECOGNIZE AND MAINTAIN THE FREEDOM of said persons.

And I hereby enjoin upon the people so declared to be free, to abstain from all violence, UNLESS IN NECESSARY SELF-DEFENCE, and I recommend to them that in all cases, when allowed, they LABOR FAITHFULLY FOR REASONABLE WAGES.

And I further declare and make known that such persons of suitable condition will be received into the armed service of the United States, to garrison forts, positions, stations, and other places, and to man vessels of all sorts in said service.

And upon this act, SINCERELY BELIEVED TO BE AN ACT OF JUSTICE, warranted by the Constitution, upon military necessity, I invoke the considerate judgment of mankind, and the gracious favor of ALMIGHTY GOD.

In testimony whereof I have hereunto set my name, and caused the seal of the United States to be affixed.

[L. S.]   Done at the CITY OF WASHINGTON, this first day of January, in the year of our Lord one thousand eight hundred and sixty-three, and of the Independence of the United States the eighty-seventh.

A. Lincoln

By the President.

William H. Seward
Secretary of State.

Entered according to Act of Congress, in the year 1864, by E. A. DIMMICK, in the Clerk's Office of the District Court of the United States for the Southern District of New York.

W. ROBERTS, Del.   C. A. ALVORD, Printer.

CHAPTER ONE

⌒

From the Civil War to Civil Rights

William Edward Burghardt Du Bois was born on February 23, 1868, in Great Barrington, Massachusetts, three years after the end of the American Civil War. During the war, slaves were officially declared free with the Emancipation Proclamation on January 1, 1863. Before he was born, the Du Bois family made their home in the North, which meant that, as African Americans, they had always been free. Northern States had abolished slavery after the American Revolution, but free blacks in the North made up a very small population. In 1860, the year the Civil War commenced, they numbered approximately 225,000. Although conditions were better because they were not enslaved, African Americans still experienced **discrimination** and **segregation** in the North.

The famous Emancipation Proclamation issued by Abraham Lincoln freed slaves in states not a part of the Union (the South).

The Civil War and Reconstruction

While Du Bois did not experience the war, he grew up during Reconstruction. After the Civil War, Reconstruction was the federal government's attempt to reunite the North and the South and to allow the southern states to return to the full union of the United States. Many Northerners wanted the South to be punished. There were many ideas and strategies that the federal government considered as to how the United States would be reconstructed. President Abraham Lincoln's own reconstruction plan required 10 percent of the voting population of the southern states to swear allegiance to the United States of America. Northerners criticized President Lincoln's plan as too lenient on the South. Southern states were struggling to rebuild after the war and needed good governance. Unfortunately, Lincoln could not see his plan through. He was **assassinated** and passed away on April 15, 1865. He left behind a country in need of a leader to bring the North and the South together.

After Lincoln's assassination, President Andrew Johnson had a different idea for Reconstruction. He favored an easy path for southern states to return to the union. Johnson was not concerned with healing the country but was primarily concerned with ensuring that white citizens retained power. Eventually, Congress passed the Reconstruction Acts of 1867, overriding President Johnson's **vetoes**, which laid out the official plan for Reconstruction and established the **Freedmen's Bureau**, the nation's first federal poverty program. Andrew Johnson was successfully **impeached** due to his opposition to the Reconstruction Acts. In fact, his impeachment came the day before Du Bois was born.

Congress's Reconstruction plan divided the formerly confederate states into five military districts to be occupied by federal troops, which the South didn't like. Congress felt this would help ensure better treatment for the newly freed black citizens. To be readmitted into the Union, each state was required to accept the Fourteenth Amendment by incorporating it into their own state constitutions.

The Thirteenth, Fourteenth, and Fifteenth Amendments to the Constitution were passed in the years following the Civil War. All three were written to ensure that black Americans were considered citizens of the United States and afforded equal political rights. The Thirteenth Amendment began as the Emancipation Proclamation on January 1, 1863, when President Lincoln declared all slaves in Confederate states to be free. Although regarded as a very important declaration, the Emancipation Proclamation was limited because it only applied to states that **seceded** from the Union and it was difficult to enforce. The Thirteenth Amendment successfully and legally abolished slavery for the entire United States of America. The House finally passed it on January 31, 1865, and it was officially **ratified** by all the states nearly two years later, on December 18, 1865. Many states resisted ratifying the amendment because they didn't want African Americans to have the same rights as whites.

Both the Fourteenth and Fifteenth Amendments took years to be ratified by all the states, even though ratifying the amendments would allow the southern states back into the United States. The Fourteenth and Fifteenth Amendments granted citizenship and voting rights to black men and overall protection of basic civil rights for freedmen. However, African Americans continued to fight for their rights even after the passage of these amendments, and it would be many years before Du Bois traveled to the south and learned about its entrenched **racism** and segregation.

Postbellum Life in the North

Du Bois's hometown of Great Barrington, Massachusetts was more sympathetic to racial equality than many areas in the South. Its citizens tended to see the passing of the Reconstruction Acts as part of good Christian progress and a continuation of the **abolition** movement from before the Civil War. The town did have its own sense of hierarchy and ethnic challenges, however. Most residents of Great Barrington were Anglo-Saxon Protestants, who often had

The Civil War was bloody and brutal, but the struggle for all citizens, black and white, continued long after the surrender.

tense relationships with Catholic immigrants. For example, the earlier Dutch residents of the town began joining the Episcopal Church to separate themselves from the Irish Catholics who were arriving to work in the textile and paper mills.

At the end of the Civil War, Great Barrington had 3,920 residents. Du Bois's own research and town hall records reveal that there were approximately thirty African-American families in the Great Barrington region at that time. Generally, the black residents of Great Barrington did not work in the mills or factories. Instead, the majority of them worked on farms. A few families even owned property. Outside of farm work, the black residents tended to work in personal service as barbers, stewards, or coachmen.

Education, however, provided an unexpected opportunity for the black residents of Great Barrington, and it was an opportunity that Du Bois was able to seize. Prior to Du Bois's first birthday, the citizens of Great Barrington voted to use $2,000 to create a public high school. Up until that point, the only high schools in the town were private institutions for the affluent citizens of the area. Higher education was not a guarantee, unless you wanted to pay for it. In 1869, the public Great Barrington high school was built—it was only the second brick structure in the town.

Du Bois's high school principal, Frank Hosmer, believed in equality and positive race relations—even without the government's endorsement through Reconstruction. Hosmer was part of an old New England family with a strong **Congregationalist** faith, and he was always on the lookout for African-American leadership and talent. It wouldn't be until later in his life that Du Bois understood how influential and rare Hosmer's influence was. In the United States in the 1880s, not even sons of white mill owners regularly pursued a college education.

When Du Bois entered high school in 1881, Reconstruction had formally ended four years earlier with the Compromise of 1877. Formal **disenfranchisement** and the institutionalizing of

EDDIKASHUN QUALIFUKASHUN.

THE BLAKMAN ORTER BE EDDIKATED AFORE HE KIN VOTE WITH US WITES.

MR. 'SOLID SOUTH'

THE COLOR LINE STILL EXISTS—IN THIS CASE.

An editorial cartoon: the white man attempts to set up rules for voting including education, as his rules demonstrate his own ignorance. Grandfather clauses, literacy tests, and poll taxes were often used to keep blacks from the polls.

Jim Crow laws, banning black people from establishments and public places, were beginning to take hold, mainly in the South. Blacks were kept from voting by poll taxes, literacy tests, and **grandfather clauses**. The grandfather clause only allowed a citizen to vote if his grandfather had been allowed to vote. Because it had previously been illegal for African Americans to vote, most African Americans, although legally allowed to vote now, were blocked from doing so because their grandfathers had been disenfranchised, too.

College Life in the South

As Du Bois went off to college at Fisk University in Nashville, Tennessee, he became immersed in segregation and the Jim Crow South. When Du Bois attended Fisk, Jim Crow laws had not reached their full effect, but Du Bois soon learned the South's true racial culture. He wrote in his autobiography, "Murder, killing, and maiming Negroes, raping Negro women—in the 80s and in the southern South, this was not even news; it got no publicity, it caused no arrest; and punishment for such transgression was so unusual that the fact was telegraphed North." Segregation, **lynching**, and other effects of the Jim Crow laws would make Du Bois's desire for research and activism even more important.

His first experience with segregation was likely on the train to Tennessee to attend Fisk. On this journey, he would have had to ride in the Jim Crow car. The Jim Crow car was the only place blacks were allowed in the train, and it was likely crowded, dirty, and not well maintained. Tennessee was the first state to enact race separation laws in public spaces in 1881. These laws were then upheld with the 1896 Supreme Court ruling in the case of *Plessy v. Ferguson*. In *Plessy v. Ferguson,* the Court upheld the legality of segregation and the idea of "separate but equal." In other words, segregation was legal as long as the facilities being segregated were equal for both blacks and whites. This rarely happened, however, and segregation usually meant substandard and dirty accommodations for blacks.

The full effects of segregation and the Jim Crow laws had not yet been realized when Du Bois was at Fisk. During the 1880s, the occasional black citizen was elected to the House of Representatives in states like Alabama, North Carolina, and Virginia. Poll taxes, literacy tests, and other forms of intimidation grew ever more popular, but black men were still voting. In Louisiana, despite the attempts to keep blacks from voting, 130,344 black men were registered to vote. In fact, at this time, students at Fisk and other black universities, like Atlanta and Howard Universities, believed that as long as they were educated and productive members of society, they would be allowed to vote. Once they voted, their voices and concerns would be represented and conditions would improve.

As segregation was becoming more entrenched in the South, the lynching of black Americans also grew ever more popular while Du Bois attended Fisk. Lynching in the South violently excluded blacks from the criminal justice system. White mobs punished blacks by hanging and oftentimes burning them. Meant as an act of terror, lynching spread fear among blacks as a way to maintain **white supremacy**. Lynching had existed prior to Reconstruction but it gained momentum as blacks gained more political and economic freedom in the South. Between 1882 and 1951, it is conservatively estimated that 4,730 people were lynched. Approximately 72 percent of those lynched were black. During this time, the majority of lynchings took place in Mississippi, Georgia, Texas, Louisiana, and Alabama.

Because of this extreme **vigilante** justice, many Fisk students would only leave campus and go into the city of Nashville if they were armed. Once Du Bois was simply walking down the street when he accidentally brushed against a white woman. He doffed his hat in apology, a gesture which would have been acceptable in Great Barrington. The woman exploded, became red-faced, and shouted expletives at him. In his *Darkwater* autobiography, Du Bois notes that the incident was the last time he ever intentionally doffed his hat at a white woman. The experience scared Du Bois. It was not uncommon for a lynch mob to seek justice for something as accidental as a black man bumping into a white woman.

Living and Working in the South

One of the contributing economic factors to the Civil War was the difference in Northern and Southern industries. The North's economy was based on manufacturing. The South's economy, however, was less developed. It was based on the plantation system and agriculture. The differing needs of the two regions led to increased conflict and contributed to the secession of Southern states from the United States of America.

According to many historians, the withdrawal of federal troops from the South in 1877 was a turning point for industry and growth in the South. Atlanta, Du Bois's future home, had only fourteen thousand residents when Union General William T. Sherman marched through the city in 1864 near the end of the Civil War. By 1880, however, Atlanta had a population of forty thousand—and it just kept growing. Manufacturing, especially in the textile and iron industries, grew rapidly. More blacks than ever before began working in factories due to increased demand, but they were still primarily employed in agriculture.

One of the symbols of increased work opportunities at the time was the 1895 Atlanta Exposition. The exposition included exhibits on the latest technology and a whole room devoted to the progress of black Americans. Booker T. Washington was the keynote speaker and gave his famous "Atlanta Compromise" speech. The speech itself was controversial among many black activists because it advocated for the acceptance of white rule over African Americans, but it did encourage industrial leaders of the South to hire black workers.

The opening up of more industrial jobs for blacks did not provide them with more rights and opportunities. Instead, segregation only grew stronger toward the end of the century. Du Bois experienced the most stringent segregation of his life when he and his family

New York City drew many African Americans. Although life was often just as hard as it was in the South, small things like integrated public transportation were a draw.

moved to Atlanta, beginning in 1897. Although Atlanta University was one of the premier institutions in the South and in Atlanta, much of the city itself was not accessible to Du Bois. For example, taxpayer money built a new, state-of-the-art public library in Atlanta, but blacks were forbidden to use it. In addition, the transportation system of Atlanta was segregated. In protest, many black residents chose not to use it, like Du Bois and his wife, Nina. Because they did not use Atlanta's public transportation, they only had access to a small section of Atlanta that they could walk to for their shopping and entertainment. Du Bois was able to suffer this segregation because he was immersed in his work and the university community. His wife, Nina, however, absolutely hated living in Atlanta due to the segregation.

Race Riots

In 1906, from September 22 through the 24, a horrific race **riot** occurred in Atlanta. Prior to midnight on September 22, a mob of twenty-two thousand white people set out to beat every single black person they found on the streets. With this violent goal, the riot lasted for two days. At the busiest intersection in Atlanta, Five Points, the mob essentially shut down the public transportation system and plucked black patrons off electric streetcars. Some riders were simply thrown from the cars, while others were assaulted and beaten with clubs or pelted with stones. The *Atlanta Constitution* reported that some of the streets of Atlanta were running red with the blood of African Americans who had been attacked. By the end of the riot, twenty-five African Americans had been killed, as well as two European Americans.

Four alleged assaults on white women by black men reported in Atlanta newspapers on September 22 supposedly caused this riot. The actual underlying cause was class conflict among the white residents of Atlanta. Whites, wealthy or not, felt jobs should go to whites, not blacks, and banded together to ensure this. Blacks were targeted because they were a growing labor reserve that increasingly demanded the right to vote and a better education system. Successful black Atlanta residents were a threat to the city's poor, white residents. The only thing poor whites could use to prevent losing jobs and status was their skin color. When the *New York Times* asked the Atlanta mayor about the cause of the riot, he firmly blamed black men for assaulting white women and justified the rioters' actions.

Du Bois was out of town when the riot began and, upon hearing about it, he rushed home to protect his wife and daughter. Although generally opposed to violence, he purchased a shotgun. He sat on the steps outside the hall where they lived with the gun, determined to protect his home, his family, and his university. The Atlanta riot would not drastically change the existing racial tensions in Atlanta

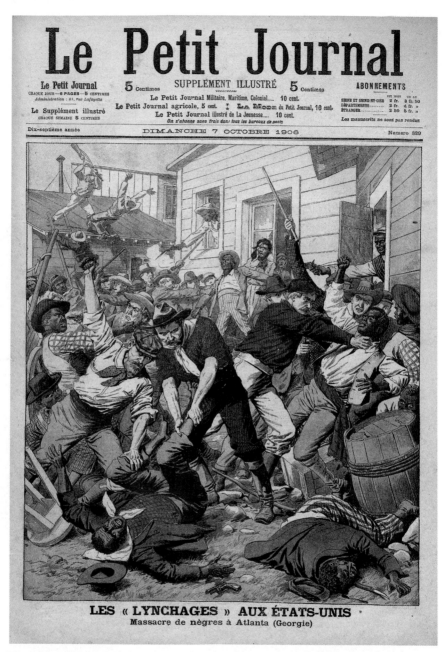

Le Petit Journal

| Le Petit Journal | 5 Centimes | SUPPLÉMENT ILLUSTRÉ | 5 Centimes | ABONNEMENTS |

CHAQUE JOUR—8 PAGES—5 CENTIMES
Administration : 61, rue Lafayette

Le Petit Journal Militaire, Maritime, Colonial..... 10 cent.
Le Petit Journal agricole, 5 cent. ‡ LA MODE du Petit Journal, 10 cent.

Le Supplément illustré
CHAQUE SEMAINE 5 CENTIMES

Le Petit Journal illustré de La Jeunesse.... 10 cent.
On s'abonne sans frais dans tous les bureaux de poste

	SIX MOIS	UN AN
SEINE ET SEINE-ET-OISE	2 fr.	3 fr. 50
DÉPARTEMENTS	2 fr.	4 fr. »
ÉTRANGER	2 50	5 fr. »

Les manuscrits ne sont pas rendus

Dix-septième année   **DIMANCHE 7 OCTOBRE 1906**   Numéro 829

LES « LYNCHAGES » AUX ÉTATS-UNIS
Massacre de nègres à Atlanta (Georgie)

The cover of the October 7, 1906 issue of *Le Petit Journal* depicts the brutal Atlanta massacre that Du Bois himself witnessed.

The March on Washington, a historic moment for African Americans and Dr. Martin Luther King Jr., coincided with Du Bois's passing.

THE MARCH ON
WASHINGTON

On August 28, 1963, over two hundred thousand Americans gathered in Washington, DC for a political rally now called the March on Washington but the official title of which was the March on Washington for Jobs and Freedom. The rally was planned by a variety of civil rights organizations, including the NAACP and the SCLC, to advocate for the passage of the Civil Rights Act, which would make discrimination based on race, color, sex, or religion illegal. The march was a success and included a full day of speeches and songs from people like Dr. King, John Lewis, Mahalia Jackson, and Bob Dylan. Most notably, it was the day that Dr. King gave his famous "I Have a Dream" speech. The speech has since become a readily accessible summary of the highest aspirations of the civil rights movement.

The march itself wasn't immediately successful. Congress didn't pass the Civil Rights Act until 1964, and the Voting Rights Act became law in 1965. The March on Washington occurred on the same day that Du Bois passed away.

or in the South; it was simply another agitation in a long list of racial disturbances and riots. After the riot was over and his family was safe, Du Bois documented the riot and his anger in the impassioned poem, "Litany of Atlanta."

Another riot that directly affected Du Bois's life trajectory occurred on August 14, 1908, in Springfield, Illinois. The riot was sparked by the alleged rape of the white wife of a railway worker by a black man. Like the Atlanta riots, this alleged rape caused a riot, although the rioting was really in response to ongoing tensions related to the demographics and economics of the area. Springfield's population was about ten percent black but steadily growing. Many of the blacks who were settling in Springfield were prosperous, as well.

The actual violence of the riot led to approximately eighty injuries, six fatal shootings, two lynchings and $200,000 in damage. Two thousand black residents fled the city before the National Guard restored order. Springfield is also the city where President Abraham Lincoln was born and then buried upon his death. The white mob used Lincoln in their rallying cry. They ran through the streets shouting, "Lincoln freed you; we'll show you where you belong!" Reporters for the *Illinois State Journal* stated that the causes of the riot did not stem from hatred towards blacks, but rather the black residents' own sense of inferiority. Just as with the Atlanta riot, the black community was blamed for the one in Springfield. This punctuated the fact that racial tensions and discrimination were not just a regional issue, playing out in the South. Instead, national leaders were forced to acknowledge that racism and race relations were a problem throughout the whole United States of America. From the moment of the Springfield riot onward, civil rights activists like Mary White Ovington and William Walling were galvanized and angry. This would inspire them to cofound the NAACP with W. E. B. Du Bois.

The Great Migration

Segregation, lynching, and a lack of good jobs and educational opportunities all worked together to push many blacks to find new opportunities in the North. Despite the hope of an industrializing South, which would lead to better jobs for African Americans, by the end of the nineteenth century little progress was made toward racial justice. The majority of black farmers were **sharecroppers**, or tenant farmers, with very little right to the fruits of their labors. Oftentimes at the end of a season, sharecroppers might find themselves more in debt to the plantation owner and with no choice but to continue farming. The job opportunities that Washington touted—much to Du Bois's dismay—weren't necessarily real.

In addition to the lack of economic opportunities in the South, blacks had new ideas about how to live their lives. The generation of former slaves was growing older and passing away, and younger generations of African Americans were discontent with the few opportunities white society provided them. The prevalence of lynchings also added a constant sense of terror for those living in the South.

At the turn of the nineteenth century, many blacks began migrating to the North, beginning their exodus from the South. Around 1890, those leaving the South were generally educated and leaving the South for cities like New York and Chicago. Later in the century, especially once World War I began, there were few immigrants from Europe coming into the northern cities and, thus, there were plenty of job opportunities for blacks. By 1930, over two million blacks had migrated to cities in the North. Many saw the opportunity to move north as an opportunity to get to the Promised Land. However, the North was not what they had hoped it to be, and many of the same political and economic challenges awaited them in the northern cities, as well.

Regardless, the North was where many migrating black Southerners placed their expectations. World War I provided many new opportunities and a demand for labor. Black men began working in factories and manufacturing instead of domestic and personal services. Black women primarily worked as domestic servants, but they were breaking into the garment industry, as well. Wages gradually increased during this time and there were more and more opportunities for college-educated, professional African Americans in the urban North.

The Harlem Renaissance

Due in part to the Great Migration, black artists, writers, and entertainers converged on New York City, and specifically on Harlem. Du Bois was already in New York and working as the editor for the NAACP's magazine, the *Crisis*. An artistic explosion—creating literature and other materials that were distinctly nonwhite—took place from 1917 until about 1935 and became known as the Harlem Renaissance. *The New Negro*, an anthology of essays, poems, art, short stories, and songs by black artists and edited by Alain Locke, became the flagship accomplishment of the movement. Authors like Zora Neale Hurston, Langston Hughes, and Claude McKay were featured for their short fiction and poetry. Du Bois's essay "The Negro Mind Reaches Out" was also included in this anthology. *The New Negro* represented and rallied the black individual who would no longer submit to the discrimination of racial segregation. In the title essay of the anthology, Locke wrote of a new consciousness in the wake of the Great Migration and the talent descending on Harlem. He recognized the tradition of African-American art in music and folk art and called for a new wave of artistic creations. The biggest challenge for black artists in the Harlem Renaissance was to create a distinct and unique body of work that was still recognizably African American.

Alain Locke, quintessential writer and editor of the Harlem Renaissance, sits at his desk at Howard University in Washington, DC.

Du Bois, although not physically located in Harlem, was in conversation with many of the artists of the time and contributed his own works to the Renaissance. Although he did write some fiction, his essays and literary criticism were his most important contributions. In his 1926 essay, "Criteria of Negro Art," Du Bois recognized and encouraged the creation of unique black art forms as a way to further express African Americans' full citizenship and personhood. The Harlem Renaissance was a way for unique artistic expression to take place alongside the growing discontent over discrimination, disenfranchisement, and lack of educational opportunities.

The Civil Rights Movement

The NAACP was officially founded in 1909 and spent its early years building its reputation and fighting segregation, often in the court system. The 1920s, with the advent of the NAACP and the burgeoning arts movement called the Harlem Renaissance, seemed like the start of a new era—an era in which blacks were guaranteed the right to vote and attend quality public schools. Legally, however, segregation would remain in place for the duration of Du Bois's life.

The first turning point in the modern civil rights movement came in 1954, less than ten years before Du Bois's death. The Supreme Court's *Brown v. Board of Education of Topeka, Kansas* ruling declared that segregation and the "separate but equal" doctrine were both illegal. The NAACP led the litigation efforts that had public school segregation declared unconstitutional. However, black activism was still needed to compel the federal government to implement the decision and order all public schools to submit to the legal mandate of integration. The 1950s and 1960s included many NAACP-sponsored lawsuits that grew out of the *Brown v. Board of Education* ruling.

Another milestone in black activism began on December 1, 1955, with the Montgomery Bus Boycott. Rosa Parks, a resident of

Montgomery, Alabama, refused to give up her seat on the bus to a white rider. Parks was jailed, and the black community launched a boycott of the city's buses that lasted over a year. Martin Luther King Jr. became one of the country's most prominent civil rights leaders as a result of this **boycott**. Both King and Parks were members of the NAACP, but they soon helped found a new protest organization in 1957 called the Southern Christian Leadership Conference (SCLC).

King, along with other organizers, initiated several other protests in subsequent years. Beginning on February 1, 1960, in North Carolina, student **sit-ins** to end segregation at lunch counters were implemented and soon spread throughout the South. There were countless other boycotts and marches, throughout the South especially. The ratification of the Civil Rights and Voting Rights Acts, occurring in the years surrounding Du Bois's death, was the legal realization of the Fourteenth and Fifteenth Amendments, which were ratified in the early days of Du Bois's life.

CHAPTER TWO

⌒

The Long Life
of Du Bois

When Du Bois was born on February 23, 1868, his birth certificate read "William E. Duboise," an obvious misspelling. To the people of Great Barrington, he was called Willie. He was the only child of Mary Silvina Burghardt, a longtime resident of Great Barrington, and Alfred Du Bois. Mary was already thirty-six years old at the time of his birth—she and Alfred had married just a year previously in the nearby village of Housatonic. She worked as a domestic servant, and her parents disapproved of her marriage to the often-unemployed Alfred. By the time Du Bois had his first birthday, Alfred had left town.

Alfred Du Bois was born in Haiti and came to the United States sometime before 1860. Census records show that he was in upstate New York in 1860, likely working as a barber, cook, or waiter before enlisting in the Union Army in Poughkeepsie, New York. He did not maintain his service throughout the Civil

A young W. E. B. Du Bois poses for
a portrait in 1872, at age four.

War, however, and he was listed as a deserter. Du Bois's own accounts of his father provide contradictory accounts of where Alfred lived, when he died, and what kind of person he was. The Burghardts never talked about Alfred, and Du Bois recognized that his father was not well-liked by the Burghardt clan.

The Burghardt family was not wealthy, but they had a lot of history in Great Barrington and in the United States. Du Bois's maternal great-grandfather, Jack Burghardt, is rumored to have been involved with Shay's Rebellion and the War of 1812. Jack's father, Tom, is supposed to have served in the Continental Army during the Revolutionary War, possibly in exchange for his freedom. The Burghardts were modest farmers and semi-skilled laborers who took great pride in respectability. Good moral behaviors were very important to them, and they boasted that, over the course of three generations, there had only been one child born out of wedlock—and that child was Du Bois's own elder half-brother, Adelbert. Adelbert was born in 1862 outside of Great Barrington, and he and Du Bois did not have a close relationship.

When Du Bois was five, Othello Burghardt, the family patriarch, died, and the family began to struggle even more financially. Du Bois lived with his mother and his aunt Sarah, along with his brother and another cousin, above the stables of an estate. The home was near the school in the center of Great Barrington, which Du Bois loved. After his aunt Sarah died in 1875, the family moved to Railroad Street— and lived in extreme poverty. Railroad Street was located near the tracks, as the name suggests, and housed the saloons, gambling dens, and at least one brothel. Du Bois's family lived in a rundown house that they shared with another destitute, white family.

Soon after renting the house on Railroad Street, Du Bois's mother suffered a paralytic stroke. Mary lost the full use of her left leg and arm, which rendered her disabled and less employable. Du Bois and his mother were assisted as much as possible by his Uncle James, who worked as a barber, and his aunts. Other townspeople provided them with the necessities for living when they could and employed Mary in the few light chores and odd jobs that she could handle. Du Bois and his brother, Adelbert, also pitched in. Adelbert was already living away from home and working in Albany, and he sent home what money he could. Du Bois picked up any odd jobs he could. He also helped his mother every day after school, meeting her to carry her bundles and helping her walk home. During an interview, Du Bois recalled that townspeople would commend him for being nice to his mother, which always struck him as an odd compliment. Du Bois explained that he was raised to be helpful, and that he and his mother were simply companions.

Du Bois's mother, Mary, knew that life had few opportunities for her as a poor, uneducated, disabled, black woman, and so she invested everything she could in her son. She gave Du Bois certain rules to help him succeed. The rules forbid him from touching liquor, getting involved with loose women, gambling, or smoking. Other than that, she left Du Bois to his own devices. One of her greatest pleasures was Du Bois's performance in school. As Du Bois began to realize that performing well in school pleased his mother, he also recognized that his academic success could improve their lives. Eventually, his mother moved the two of them into a small property near the river, away from Railroad Street. They boarded with Du Bois's uncle James, the barber, and for the first time in his life Du Bois had his own room, although the house did not have electricity or plumbing.

Racism in Great Barrington

With the move to the small house near the river came more responsibility for Du Bois. He did every odd job possible to help contribute to the family's living expenses. He mowed lawns, distributed tea at the new A&P chain, delivered papers, chopped wood, stoked stoves in the morning for various businesses, and gathered milk from the cows.

Du Bois also learned a great deal as a writer while still in high school. In April 1883, Du Bois's first piece was published in the

New York Globe, a progressive black publication founded by an African-American man named Timothy Thomas Fortune. Du Bois greatly admired Fortune, one of the first black men outside of his own family whom he aspired to be like. Du Bois had been the Great Barrington paper boy for about a year before the article appeared. Between April 10, 1883, and May 16, 1885, Du Bois published twenty-four articles, signed W.E.D., in the *Globe*. He also had the opportunity to write for the *Springfield Republican* as an occasional correspondent from Great Barrington. As he worked at various odd jobs, Du Bois began to recognize how black residents in Great Barrington were treated poorly.

Although Du Bois wouldn't experience the harsh racism of the South until college, at the age of thirteen he admitted to having days of crying in secret because of how he was treated. He had begun to realize that every black family in the town was poorer than any white family. Furthermore, Du Bois recognized that many white citizens saw his brown skin as a symbol of misfortune or as something to fear. At one point, Du Bois was nearly sent away to a reform school for stealing grapes from the yard of a wealthy citizen. Principal Hosmer advocated for him and Du Bois was able to pursue his hallmark education, instead of heading to reform school and down a different path.

A Great Barrington Education

As Du Bois grew and continued to do well in school, certain Great Barrington citizens began taking an interest in him and his education. He was the favorite student of the stern Miss Cross in primary school. Du Bois was the only black student in his school, but he learned quickly and advanced faster than his white classmates.

Du Bois's high school education was a first for both the town and the Burghardt family. Prior to Du Bois attending the new Great Barrington high school, only one or two black teenagers had taken a year or so of classes at the school, and no Burghardt had

Du Bois, as a young man, learned the value of education in Great Barrington.

ever received more than an elementary school education. When Du Bois first enrolled in high school, he thought that the best way to support himself and his mother, and to use his education, was to immerse himself in all the **vocational** courses offered at Great Barrington High. This way he could get a more advanced labor-based job. Instead, Principal Hosmer suggested that college preparatory classes might serve him better and encouraged Du Bois to take a more academic path. Principal Hosmer even spoke to a local mill owner about sponsoring Du Bois and buying all the necessary and expensive textbooks. With Hosmer's support and Du Bois's own inherent sense of proving something to the world, he pursued his education wholeheartedly.

No official academic records survive of Du Bois's time at Great Barrington High, but he apparently achieved extremely good grades while he was enrolled. His commencement was held in the town hall on June 27, 1884, and he graduated with six other boys and six girls. Du Bois delivered an oration on Wendell Phillips, a prominent figure in the abolition movement. The *Berkshire Courier,* the local paper, gave an account of the ceremony and noted that Du Bois's address drew much applause.

Prior to graduation, Du Bois had started dreaming about going to Harvard. Ever since Hosmer had encouraged him to prepare for college instead of vocational school, Du Bois was focused on Harvard. Williams College, in nearby Williamstown, Massachusetts, was the more realistic option for Du Bois to attend, but he didn't end up enrolling there, either. In addition to the monetary challenges of attending either school, Du Bois couldn't leave his mother, who needed more care than ever. After graduation, Du Bois stayed in Great Barrington to work and care for his mother. He was only sixteen and felt that there was still plenty of time for college. Du Bois understood as a sixteen year old what his mother had sacrificed on his behalf. Later in life he wrote the essay "The Damnation of Women" and noted the sad truth that "[o]nly at the sacrifice of intelligence and the chance to do their best work can the majority of modern women bear children." Despite his understanding of his mother's sacrifices, he didn't have to sacrifice his ambitions for

The Great Barrington High class of 1884, including Du Bois, who delivered an oration at the commencement address.

too long. Unfortunately, his mother died of an apoplectic stroke in March 1885.

Du Bois Heads South

Du Bois's mother's death did not free him to pursue his dream of Harvard right away. Although the Great Barrington community rallied around him, it was not to send him to Harvard. In *Darkwater,* Du Bois writes, "Harvard was the goal of my dreams, but my white friends hesitated and my black friends were silent." Instead, four area Congregational churches pledged twenty-five dollars apiece to pay for Du Bois's education at Fisk University. Fisk University, located in Nashville, Tennessee, was a Congregational school for black students founded in 1866. Today, it is still a predominantly black school and the oldest institution of higher learning in Nashville. Although Du Bois was disappointed he wasn't heading to Harvard, he viewed living in the South as an adventure in which he could learn more

Du Bois and his Fisk University classmates, circa 1888.

HARVARD APPLICATION

Dated October 29, 1887, the following is Du Bois's application letter to Harvard:

"Dear Sir:

I am a Negro, a student of Fisk University. I shall receive the degree of A.B. from this institution next June at the age of 20. I wish to pursue at Harvard a course of study for the degree of Ph.D. in Political Science after graduation. I am poor and if I should enter your college next year would probably not be able to raise more [than] $100 or 150. If I should teach a year and then enter I could earn enough to pay my expenses for a year. I wish your advice as to what I had better do. You can see by the catalogue I shall send herewith what our course of instruction is here. I can furnish satisfactory certificates of character and scholarship from the President and Professors of Fisk, and from Western Massachusetts where I was born, and graduated from the Public Schools. I am also Editor of the *Fisk Herald*. As I said I wish your advice as to whether I had better teach a year or two or come immediately after graduation. I expect to take the special field of Political Economy."

about the black community. Du Bois recognized the inequality of blacks and whites in Great Barrington, but he had no experience with the extreme racism and segregation in the South. Beyond a trip to meet his grandfather, he had had very little interaction with the larger black community outside of Great Barrington.

Fisk definitely provided Du Bois with a connection to the larger black community. The history of Fisk, which had opened on the site of a Union army hospital after the Civil War, was impressive. In its early years, Fisk was known as the Fisk Free Colored School, and two hundred ex-slaves came to learn on its opening day. When Du Bois arrived approximately twenty-five years later, Fisk was the nation's most famous college for educating African-American students. Fisk fought against many of the prevailing attitudes at the time, including that blacks should only be educated for labor and vocational training. Their curriculum included Greek, Latin, French, German, theology, natural sciences, music, moral philosophy, and history. When Du Bois arrived in 1885, he enrolled in the sophomore class because his Great Barrington High education was advanced enough to allow him to skip ahead.

While at Fisk, Du Bois didn't just focus on his studies and academic pursuits. He wanted to be immersed in Southern culture and meet as many African Americans as possible—especially those who would never see the inside of a university classroom. Instead of returning to Great Barrington at the end of his first year at Fisk, he went to Lebanon Pike, a town outside of Nashville, and enrolled in a week-long course at Lebanon Teachers' Institute. He then passed an examination—an extremely primitive one at that—and became a certified elementary school teacher. That summer, Du Bois taught school in Wilson County, Tennessee, approximately fifty miles from Nashville. He also returned the following summer to teach and learn.

In addition to rigorously pursuing his studies at Fisk, Du Bois joined a men's choir and became acquainted with African-American spirituals. He also worked as an editor at the *Fisk Herald* newspaper. His editorials included adulating his hero Timothy Thomas Fortune as he retired from the *Globe*, enthusiastically supporting **feminism**, and reflecting on the duty of the nation to protect the rights of Fisk students. Although he never had an easy camaraderie with his peers, by the end of his time at Fisk, Du Bois was beginning to fit in with the other students and was even becoming popular. He even dated his first real girlfriend, Nellie.

Making History at Harvard

Prior to graduating from Fisk, Du Bois was accepted to Harvard University for graduate school with a scholarship. After graduating from Fisk, Du Bois was supposed to be Harvard-bound in the fall of 1888. However, the finances needed to get him to Harvard were still in question. Another student at Fisk encouraged Du Bois to work as a waiter at a Minnesota resort hotel. Du Bois worked in Lake Minnetonka during the summer of 1888 and made enough money to finally attend Harvard, despite the fact that he didn't earn a tip the whole summer as a waiter. He experienced racism in a whole new way in Minnesota—in a less obvious way than in the Jim Crow South.

Despite earning admittance to the prestigious university, Du Bois was a Harvard student in only the most basic of ways—he was a student but not a true member of the community. One of 282 members of the class of 1890, he was only the seventh black American to be admitted in the history of school. Du Bois took advantage of all the educational resources that the school could offer, but his social life was segregated. In his autobiography, Du Bois recognized that he was able to accept this segregation after living in the South. Had he attended Harvard immediately after graduating Great Barrington High, he would have sought the companionship of white students and ended up even more disappointed.

Although Du Bois didn't have the camaraderie of the average Harvard student, he excelled academically. Du Bois wrote of his experience at Harvard: "I asked nothing of Harvard but the tutelage of teachers and the freedom of the laboratory and library." He immersed himself in the philosophy department and found a mentor

After earning his master's degree in 1890, Du Bois poses with his Harvard classmates.

in William James and other faculty members. Eventually, Du Bois chose to pursue history instead of philosophy, because he believed it provided even more job opportunities. He was one of six speakers at his graduate commencement. After earning his master's degree in history in 1892, Du Bois focused on pursuing his next dream, to study in Europe.

The End of Du Bois's Formal Education

DuBois desired a degree from a German university, which both he and the academic world still saw as far superior to a Harvard degree. Max Weber, a famous sociologist, was in Berlin and, upon arriving at Friedrich Wilhelm University, Du Bois often attended his lectures. While studying in Germany, he was fully immersed in student life and didn't constantly have to face racism and the racial questions that were always so important in the United States. He was poor, but poor like other students. Unfortunately, Du Bois could not afford to reside permanently in Germany and, therefore, could not complete his PhD in Berlin because the university had a residency requirement. In some ways, Du Bois's time studying at Friedrich Wilhelm University was the pinnacle of his academic career.

Professor Du Bois

Du Bois found himself searching for a job while completing his PhD upon his return from Germany. For many teaching jobs, Du Bois was considered overqualified. Eventually, Du Bois accepted a position in the classics department at Wilberforce University in Ohio, the oldest black college in the United States. Du Bois wasn't entirely at home at Wilberforce, particularly due to its religious emphasis, but during his first academic year of teaching, he was able to complete his twelve-chapter Harvard doctoral dissertation, *The Suppression of the African Slave Trade to the United States of America, 1638-1870*. With the successful completion of the dissertation, Du Bois became the first black man to earn a PhD from Harvard.

Not long after completing his dissertation, Du Bois left Wilberforce University. He disliked the school for its excessive religiosity and, before his tenure ended there, he led at least one protest with the students against the administration. He left Wilberforce in 1896 and headed to Philadelphia's Seventh Ward to direct a sociological study of the black population for a year. The study was published as *The Philadelphia Negro: A Social Study*. With the publication of the study and his dissertation, Du Bois earned a reputation as a leading American scholar. From that point on, Du Bois was a relevant academic, writer, and activist on a national level.

After conducting his study in Philadelphia, Du Bois accepted a professorship of economics and history at Atlanta University in 1897. Atlanta University was founded in 1865 with the assistance of the Freedmen's Bureau. It was the first graduate institution for a primarily African-American student body. Atlanta became Du Bois's home base for more than a decade until he moved to New York in 1910. In 1933, he returned as a visiting professor, then served as the chair of the sociology department until he was forced to retire in 1944. While on faculty at Atlanta University, he frequently traveled to conferences as a scholar and as a speaker.

From Professor to Activist

In 1905, while still on the faculty of Atlanta University, Du Bois helped found and was elected general secretary of the Niagara Movement. The movement existed for three more meetings, the fourth of which, in 1908, was poorly attended. A precursor to the NAACP, the Niagara Movement was a protest group made up of black scholars and professionals. Later, in 1909, Du Bois helped found the NAACP. From 1910 to 1934, he served as the NAACP's director of publicity and research, a member of the board of directors, and as editor of its monthly magazine, the *Crisis.*

Over time, Du Bois's own advocacy of integration and equality evolved. In 1934, he resigned from the NAACP and began to advocate more of a **black nationalist** strategy. This stance advocated for black-controlled institutions and schools. During this phase of his life, Du Bois became increasingly frustrated by race relations—although he would return to the NAACP for a while. He continued to write, publishing an autobiography and several essay collections. Du Bois also traveled all over the world for peace conferences—from Poland to China and Japan. In 1950, he unsuccessfully ran for the US Senate as a member of the American Labor party in New York.

Du Bois's Family Life

From the death of his mother until his marriage, Du Bois focused very little on his personal life. Even once he was married, research and writing were always his first priority. While at Wilberforce University, Du Bois met a young student named Nina Gomer. In 1896, he married Nina, and the two of them moved to Philadelphia where Du Bois conducted a sociological study on the black population of Philadelphia's Seventh Ward. The two newlyweds

Du Bois and his wife, Nina, with their second child, Nina Yolande.

lived above a cafeteria and, years later, Du Bois wrote that he felt bad that their first home was in such an impoverished and dangerous area. Over the years, many speculated that Du Bois and Nina weren't the best match. Nina was very calm and quiet, the daughter of a hotel chef from Cedar Rapids, Iowa. Friends and associates often noted that she had very little to say. She did not have an academic mind like Du Bois. Although she often felt out of place intellectually, she played the part of the faculty wife very well and was an excellent host and consummate caregiver. She also vehemently hated the segregation and racism in Atlanta, where the Du Bois family spent approximately twelve years living after Philadelphia, and again for another ten years after living in New York.

Nina was generally known for her devotion to her children, the complete opposite of Du Bois, who was often gone or traveling. In October 1897, Nina gave birth to their son, Burghardt Gomer Du Bois, in Great Barrington. Unfortunately, Du Bois missed the birth due to work. For a time, the birth of their son brought Nina and Du Bois closer together than they had previously been in their marriage. Du Bois also reflected on the fact that Burghardt's birth renewed his desire to make a more equal and just country. Unfortunately, on May 24, 1899, Burghardt died of diphtheria in Atlanta. His death put a great strain on Du Bois's marriage. A little over a year later, Nina gave birth to their only daughter, Nina Yolande, on October 21, 1901. Nina Yolande was plagued with health issues throughout adulthood and she died of a heart attack in 1961, two years before her father.

Nina and Du Bois remained married until Nina's death, although the two had drifted apart much earlier. In their marriage, Du Bois had at least one confirmed affair, with Harlem Renaissance writer Jessie Redmond Fauset. Not long after his wife's death, Du Bois married Shirley Graham, a much younger writer, teacher, and activist.

The Expatriate

Du Bois's final years included a lot of world travel and increased interest in communism and the economics of the working classes. His travel to countries like the Soviet Union and China raised the suspicions of the US government. After being tried and acquitted of being an agent for a foreign state, Du Bois spent less and less time in the United States. In the late 1950s, he traveled extensively in Russia and China and officially joined the Communist Party of the United States in 1961. He moved to and became a citizen of Ghana that year, as well. Du Bois spent the final chapter of his life in Ghana, where he would die at the age of ninety-five as the March on Washington began thousands of miles away.

CHAPTER THREE

Du Bois and His Contemporaries

As a writer, Du Bois commented on the past, the present, and what he wanted the future to look like for African Americans. African-American writers and leaders that preceded him, like Timothy Thomas Fortune and Frederick Douglass, especially influenced him. During the **antebellum** period in the United States, Frederick Douglass was the preeminent black leader of the abolition movement. Born a slave in 1818, he escaped slavery and used his own story to persuade others to support abolition. Douglass gave speeches and wrote several autobiographies about his life as a slave and his escape from slavery. These narratives told his personal story but also called for the emancipation of all slaves.

Frederick Douglass, a former slave and one of Du Bois's inspirations, circa 1879.

Douglass's 1845 autobiography *Narrative of the Life of Frederick Douglass, an American Slave* became a bestseller and an important text in the abolition movement. The *Narrative* was a plea to abolitionists to outlaw slavery in the name of humanity. It sold five thousand copies within four months of publication and, by 1860 and the start of the Civil War, it had sold thirty thousand copies. Regardless of the success of the *Narrative*, Douglass was still legally a slave when the narrative was published and, with the popularity that accompanied the *Narrative,* in danger of being enslaved again. After its publication, he sailed to England and spent time there and in Ireland for a few years. While he was there, supporters raised the necessary funds to purchase his legal emancipation. He then returned to the United States.

Douglass's *Narrative* explores his life as a young slave and his formative experiences of coming to Baltimore, learning to read, and facing brutality. Douglass takes readers along on his experience in order to demonstrate how unnatural slavery was. He writes that, for much of his childhood, he lived away from his owner's plantation with his grandparents and did not inherently know that he was a slave. Eventually, he was sent to live in Baltimore. While there, one of his masters taught Douglass to read, which was illegal at the time. Both Douglass and his master would be punished for this transgression. Despite the punishments, Douglass gained something that not many other slaves could claim: he could read and write. This ability, combined with the relative freedom living in Baltimore allowed him, motivated Douglass to escape from slavery. The *Narrative* was aimed at both the hearts and minds of the reader in order to teach them the inhumanity of slavery.

Today, Douglass's narrative is seen as a cornerstone of African-American literature. His other works were continuations of his autobiography. *My Bondage and My Freedom* was published in 1855 and *Life and Times of Frederick Douglass* was published in 1881 and revised again in 1892. Many of his speeches have been published, including, most famously, "What to a slave is the 4th of

July?" Douglass was also editor and founder of the *North Star*, an abolitionist newspaper.

Douglass is most remembered for his work on behalf of abolition before the Civil War. During Reconstruction and beyond, Douglass continued to advocate, speak, and travel in the name of equal rights for former slaves. Beyond that, he advocated for equal rights for all people, including women, Native Americans, and recent immigrants. Some argued that his views were too assimilationist. Douglass urged black citizens not to create separate institutions or organizations. During the institution of Jim Crow laws, he argued that segregation would weaken the United States. Du Bois took up Douglass's arguments as he advocated for racial justice.

Douglass's autobiographies and work with the *North Star* served as an example to Du Bois. Upon Douglass's death, Du Bois was shocked and grieved for him. Douglass died on February 20, 1895, just a few hours after delivering a speech at a rally for women's rights. Du Bois was so grief-stricken, in fact, that he was compelled to write elegies to Douglass, despite not really being a poet. Du Bois wanted to write something that captured the legacy of Douglass, whom he considered the greatest of all African-American leaders and abolitionists.

Booker T. Washington

At the time of Douglass's death, Du Bois was not yet a nationally renowned activist and writer. Booker T. Washington, however, was already appealing to the masses and working on behalf of the black community. Born before the Civil War on April 5, 1856, Washington recognized the importance of an economically viable and voting black community. Like both Douglass and Du Bois, Washington was an educator, author, and orator as well as an advisor to multiple presidents of the United States. Even before Douglass's death in 1895, Washington was seen as the new dominant leader for the black community.

Washington was most famous for being the head of the Tuskegee Institute, a historically black college in Alabama founded as a black teachers' college. He wanted to challenge white supremacy through education, especially vocational education, and hard work—even at the expense of having the right to vote. For his views, Washington was commonly known as an **accommodationist**.

Washington became the principal of Tuskegee in the early 1880s at the age of only twenty-five. He ran the teachers' college and added classes on practical skills related to farming and other trades typical in the rural south. Washington valued education and many of the students earned part of their expenses though doing manual labor on the campus. With Washington at the helm, the school continued to grow, and he gradually attracted notable scholars to the school, including George Washington Carver.

In 1895, Washington gave a speech that outlined his views and would become known as the "Atlanta Compromise." For Washington, the key to blacks gaining the right to vote and full citizenship was through hard work and economic success. The key imagery of the speech was about casting down buckets. Washington encouraged blacks to "[c]ast down your buckets where you are … by making friends in every manly way of the people of all races by whom we are surrounded." To whites, he also encouraged them to cast their buckets "among these people who have, without strikes and labor wars, tilled your fields, cleared your forests, builded [sic] your railroads and cities." At the time, Du Bois agreed that economic opportunities could improve the lives of many blacks and increase sympathy from whites—although he didn't agree with everything that Washington believed. He wrote directly to Washington about their points of agreement.

Washington had a lot of power with the support of a national coalition of middle-class blacks and church leaders, as well as white philanthropists and politicians. The white philanthropists and politicians felt especially comfortable with Washington's ideas, as they didn't directly contradict their way of life. For example,

Booker T. Washington in 1903, not long after the publication of *Up From Slavery*.

BOOKER T. WASHINGTON'S
OBITUARY

Here are the opening paragraphs from the "Obituary of Booker T. Washington," written by W. E. B. Du Bois, as it appeared in the *Crisis* in December 1915:

The death of Mr. Washington marks an epoch in the history of America. He was the greatest Negro leader since Frederick Douglass, and the most distinguished man, white or black, who has come out of the South since the Civil War. His fame was international and his influence far-reaching. Of the good that he accomplished there can be no doubt: he directed the attention of the Negro race in America to the pressing necessity of economic development; he emphasized technical education and he did much to pave the way for an understanding between the white and darker races.

On the other hand there can be no doubt of Mr. Washington's mistakes and short comings: he never adequately grasped the growing bond of politics and industry; he did not understand the deeper foundations of human training and his basis of better understanding between white and black was founded on caste.

We may then generously with deep earnestness lay on the grave of Booker T. Washington testimony of our thankfulness for his undoubted help in the accumulation of Negro land and property, his establishment of Tuskegee and spreading of industrial education and his compelling of the white south to at least think of the Negro as a possible man.

On the other hand, in stern justice, we must lay on the soul of this man, a heavy responsibility for the consummation of Negro disfranchisement, the decline of the Negro college and public school and the firmer establishment of color caste in this land.

after Washington's Atlanta Compromise speech, President Grover Cleveland visited him. His prominence also later helped initiate a friendship with Andrew Carnegie, a rich, white **industrialist**, and an invitation to the White House to dine with President Theodore Roosevelt. For a while, many of the northern black leaders, especially Du Bois, reluctantly supported Washington. Even when Du Bois publicly supported the views espoused by his Atlanta Compromise, privately, Du Bois felt a lot of turmoil over Washington's beliefs. His own life path, pursuing an academic life instead of a vocational one, directly contradicted Washington's recommendation to African-American youths.

At the time, the African-American community and the public at large constantly compared Du Bois's work with Washington and his ideas. However, Du Bois was the more academically-minded thinker and the better writer—despite Washington's popular autobiography, *Up From Slavery*. Washington's autobiography was a story about faith, hard work, and overcoming adversity—and, thus, very appealing to an American audience. He used the basic slave narrative structure and form to describe his rise to prominence. With it, he argued that racial equality would come after self-reliance, surrendering the right to vote, and vocational training. While Washington described slavery as evil, he also saw it as having blessings. It is interesting to note that Washington didn't write *Up From Slavery* himself but used Max Bennett Thrasher as his ghostwriter.

Many American authors praised the book, with the first negative review coming from Du Bois in the July 16 issue of *Dial*. In the review, Du Bois argued that there was a danger in Washington's ideas, which did not provide for the enfranchisement of black citizens. Historians have noted that Du Bois's review in the *Dial* was the opening battle between Washington's views of accommodation and Du Bois and his more militant approach to guaranteeing rights for black Americans.

When Booker T. Washington died in 1915 and Du Bois wrote his obituary for the *Crisis*, many of Du Bois's contemporaries were nervous that he would not do Washington justice as a result of his own philosophical disagreements. Instead, Du Bois's final words on Washington's life were both stately and befitting of his influence, while taking a critical look at his shortcomings. He noted that Washington's passing was the end of an era in American history and that he was the greatest black leader since Frederick Douglass. Du Bois listed Tuskegee, the ideal of interracial cooperation, and his encouragement of entrepreneurship among blacks as the many things Washington contributed to the fight for racial equality. In the same obituary, Du Bois blamed Washington for the continued disenfranchisement of blacks and the decline of black colleges and public schools. According to Du Bois, Washington's strategy further implemented a color line between blacks and whites. Even with Washington's death, the two warring ideals of Du Bois and Washington persisted.

Mary White Ovington

A white woman just a few years older than Du Bois, Mary White Ovington was a civil rights advocate, social worker, scholar, and writer. Like Du Bois, she worked in many mediums. She first became involved in the campaign for civil rights after hearing Frederick Douglass speak in 1890. Ovington, as a writer, tended to write about racial problems and their economic roots. She wrote for radical and socialist journals, as well as newspapers like the *Masses* and the *New York Evening Post*. For many years, she studied employment and housing problems in the black community in Manhattan. Along the way, she was introduced to Du Bois and became familiar with his scholarship and activism.

Ovington and Du Bois were corresponding frequently by 1905. Ovington greatly admired Du Bois and his writing. At first, Du Bois simply enjoyed the admiration Ovington bestowed on him,

Mary White Ovington, researcher, educator, and one of the founding members of
the NAACP.

but he soon learned that she was an established social worker and a formidable activist. Du Bois would recommend Ovington's writing on urban, black, economic and living conditions to others by stating that she knew the most of anyone on the topic.

Ovington took her civil rights activism to the next level when she read William Walling's article on the Springfield race riot in September, 1908. She answered his call to action by writing to him and meeting up with him at his apartment in New York City. This meeting, along with a few others that would eventually also include Du Bois, led to the National Negro Committee and, eventually, the NAACP. Ovington served as a board member, executive secretary, and chairman of the NAACP. When she retired in 1947, Ovington had worked with the organization for thirty-eight years.

Ovington's familiarity with Du Bois helped him greatly. He oftentimes was quick tempered and did not like to compromise. But Ovington was able to use her knowledge of Du Bois to help in situations where ideological differences could cause tension. This was especially true in the early years of the NAACP. Ovington was a close confidante and an advisor to Du Bois—and probably the white person he was closest to during his life.

Ida B. Wells-Barnett

Ida B. Wells-Barnett, or Ida B. Wells as she is more commonly referred to, was born just a few years before Du Bois and worked as a journalist and sociologist. Wells researched and documented lynchings in the United States. Her most influential text was a hundred page pamphlet called *The Red Record* in 1895. The pamphlet catalogued and described lynchings and the struggles of blacks since the Emancipation Proclamation.

Wells and Du Bois didn't work together for many years, but they were often on the same side of issues. Wells and Du Bois both legally challenged the segregation of trains in Tennessee. Wells also denounced Washington's "Atlanta Compromise" whenever she had the chance. Wells was married to Ferdinand Barnett, the editor of

A portrait of activist and anti-lynching campaigner Ida B. Wells-Barnett around 1893.

W. E. B. Du Bois was thoroughly influenced and supported by members of his Talented Tenth as he became a prominent writer and activist.

a newspaper called the *Conservator*. The newspaper did not believe in accommodationism and had an anti-Tuskegee perspective. Both Wells and Barnett defended and promoted Du Bois's *The Souls of Black Folk* when it was published in 1903. In many ways, Wells and Du Bois did similar work, separately, but never truly worked together until the founding of the NAACP. Their later collaborations were not always smooth, but Wells was one of two African Americans (the other being Du Bois) to sign the initial call to form the NAACP. Wells would often be cast as politically radical and was often not considered for NAACP's leadership positions.

Du Bois and his Peers

In Atlanta, Du Bois had a circle of close friends who were also professors at the school. Living within the extreme segregation of Atlanta, Du Bois and his colleagues were always discussing, writing, and advocating to improve race equality. John Hope, a fellow educator and political activist, was with Du Bois at Atlanta University, and the two of them spent a lot of time debating and mulling over the racial issues of the time. Many of Du Bois's influencers and contemporaries were writers, such as the poet Paul Laurence Dunbar, the novelist Charles Waddell Chesnutt, and Jessie Fauset. Most of the contemporaries Du Bois worked with were originally urban Northerners, born between 1855 and 1875, college educated, and engaged in a profession. In fact, they formed part of what Du Bois termed the **Talented Tenth**.

As Du Bois aged and evolved, the people he surrounded himself changed, too. The leaders and advocates he worked with during the founding of the NAACP changed drastically from those he collaborated with during his work on the *Crisis* in the 1920s. From there, Du Bois's different goals and evolving views would bring him into contact with different writers taking part in the Harlem Renaissance, as well as black nationalists and members of the Communist Party.

CHAPTER FOUR

Writing and Activism

D u Bois's most significant contributions to American history are through his writing and research. He began writing early in life and spent much of his life in academia. His arguments about the need for all blacks to have the right to vote, among other equal rights issues, made him a prominent voice among early civil rights advocates. This voice led him into activism, and Du Bois spent the latter part of his life traveling and speaking. Although he was not the sole founder of the NAACP, the organization would have been much different, and perhaps less successful, without his support. *The Souls of Black Folk* and the NAACP are Du Bois's two greatest works, and they both continue to be part of the national conversation on racial identity and activism today.

Du Bois at ease, working in *The Crisis* headquarters.

The Souls of Black Folk

The Souls of Black Folk, published in 1903, came on the heels of Booker T. Washington's 1901 autobiography, *Up From Slavery*. Published on April 18, 1903, *The Souls of Black Folk* consisted of fourteen chapters that mobilized readers to find a place in history for black Americans. Historians often classify *The Souls of Black Folk* as a rebuttal to Washington's "cast down your buckets" argument. Washington argued that if blacks, especially in the South, worked hard, economic success would come to them and eventually so would voting rights and education. Du Bois vehemently disagreed that blacks should simply work hard and wait for equality. While Du Bois was motivated by his disagreements with Washington, his primary concerns when writing the essays for *Souls* were the lynchings in the South and the lack of enfranchisement for blacks, as well as the other inequalities the African-American community faced.

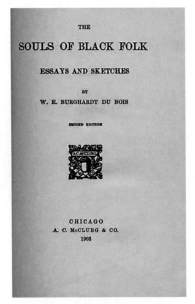

The original cover of *The Souls of Black Folk* at its publication in 1903.

The Souls of Black Folk included a variety of essays from various sources. Nine of the fourteen essays had previously appeared in publications like the *Atlantic Monthly* and the *Dial*. The essays, or chapters, varied greatly from one to another. "Of Mr. Booker T. Washington and Others," for example, was a review of Washington's *Up From Slavery* that Du Bois reworked for republication. The essay approached leadership within the black community from a different, more critical angle. In addition to critiquing Washington, whose positions and opinions were famous, Du Bois listed three critiques of failed black leadership. The five essays that had not previously been published were more literary, including

"Of the Wings of Atlanta" and "Of the Sorrow Songs." In the fifth essay, "Of the Wings of Atlanta", Du Bois peers into the politics and beliefs of the Talented Tenth, among other leaders in the movement. Not only were many of Du Bois's contemporaries opposed to Washington but, as blacks working in professional fields, they were highly offended by the suggestion that the black masses must be patient and wait for conditions to improve. Du Bois's most enduring ideas in *The Souls of Black Folk* came in the book's introduction, or "Forethought," and the first chapter, "Of Our Spiritual Strivings."

In the introduction, Du Bois introduces the veil metaphor that he uses throughout the text. The veil is representative of the division between the white and black worlds. As a black American, Du Bois explains, you are born behind the veil. The veil serves as both a symbol for mourning and a symbol for being concealed. There can be mourning for the lack of equality and justice in society. However, those who are concealed behind a veil can observe society around themselves while remaining concealed. Du Bois posited that the veil helps one see the truth of a racially-divided nation.

The first chapter, "Of Our Spiritual Strivings," explains two of Du Bois's most famous concepts, the veil—which he had introduced in the Forethought—and **double consciousness**. The revised essay begins with an excerpt from the famous spiritual, "Nobody Knows the Trouble I've Seen," which introduces all the trouble and sorrow African Americans have seen from the moment the first Africans were brought to the shores of America to work as slaves. Within the chapter, Du Bois summarizes and condenses a quarter of a century of black history. He also includes his own history as a black man and mythologizes his own experience of discovering that he is different from his white peers. Du Bois recalls his first conscious experience of racism:

> I remember well when the shadow swept across me. I was a little thing, away up in the hills of New England ... In a wee wooden schoolhouse, something put it into the

boys' and girls' heads to buy gorgeous visiting-cards—ten cents a package—and exchange. The exchange was merry, till one girl, a tall newcomer, refused my card—refused it peremptorily, without a glance. Then it dawned upon me with a certain suddenness that I was different from the others; or like, mayhap, in heart and life, and longing, but shut out from their world by a vast veil.

Young Du Bois recognized that his skin color could cause immediate discrimination. By narrating his own consciousness of racial difference, Du Bois followed writers like Frederick Douglass into an African-American literary tradition.

In the book, Du Bois also explains the problem of two-ness, or of inequality between the races, not just on a physical level but on a psychological level. Du Bois states that the problem is that the black American:

is a sort of seventh son, born with a veil, and gifted with second-sight in this American world,—a world which yields him no true self-consciousness, but only lets him see himself through the revelation of the other world ... One ever feels his two-ness—an American, a Negro; two souls, two thoughts, two unreconciled strivings.

Du Bois enumerates on the strength of the two-ness and famously coins the term double consciousness, which is defined as always seeing yourself through the eyes of others. He argues that a black person will always feel his or her warring identities. Du Bois then goes further to outline double consciousness as a strength, a capacity to see deeper truths about American society. In creating double consciousness, Du Bois draws on the traditions of the divided self from German psychology, Charles Chesnutt, Sojourner Truth, and even Ralph Waldo Emerson. Once the black American accepted and comprehended his or her true but divided self, according to Du Bois, then American society would be strengthened.

Du Bois applies the theme of two-ness in a variety of ways throughout his text. At the beginning of each essay, Du Bois includes music and lyrics from black spirituals as epigraphs. Spirituals, or sorrow songs, were the most common ways for blacks to express themselves. In each location in the text that he uses a sorrow song, a European verse from a poet like Browning or Tennyson is paired with it. With these pairings at the beginning of each chapter, Du Bois reminds his readers that without understanding and appreciating the words and songs of slaves and black people, the words and verses written by free white people are hollow. The songs and poems appear at the beginning of each essay as a representation of two Americas and of the double consciousness he was introducing to his readers.

Although much of *The Souls of Black Folk* weaves Du Bois's own personal experience throughout the essays, it is not a linear autobiography like Douglass's or Washington's. In the text, Du Bois presents himself as a scholar, historian, artist, and visionary who is trying to depict the state of black culture and look to the future. The two most famous ideas to come from *The Souls of Black Folk* are his definition of double consciousness and his accurate prediction that the greatest American problem in the twentieth century would be the problem of continued inequality for African Americans. As copies of the text continued to sell in large quantities, Du Bois's ideas and views proliferated and his popularity grew. As a result, he found himself a valuable part of the Niagara Movement and, eventually, of the NAACP—in large part due to the publication of *The Souls of Black Folk*.

The National Negro Conference

William Walling, a white labor organizer, had the inspiration to start the NAACP, not Du Bois. In 1908, the Niagara Movement fizzled out and another kind of momentum slowly began to gather.

THE NIAGARA MOVEMENT

The first Niagara Conference occurred in Ontario, Canada in 1905. The group of twenty-nine African-American men hailed from nearly every region of the country. They had planned to meet in Buffalo, New York, but after experiencing racial discrimination at the Buffalo hotel, they relocated north to Niagara Falls, Ontario. The meeting itself was not widely reported on, despite the fact that it was the first collective attempt by African Americans to demand all their rights and full citizenship. Booker T. Washington was purposely excluded from the event, and the attendees came together in opposition to Washington. From there, the meeting evolved into the creation of a new advocacy organization.

The new organization included an executive committee comprised of chairmen from each Niagara state chapter. In addition to the executive committee, ten other committees were created, including a Press and Public Opinion Committee—of which Du Bois was a member. Annual membership dues were set at five dollars. As the logistics proceeded, Du Bois was elected general secretary. From there, Du Bois, with assistance, drafted a document outlining the wrongs inflicted on the black citizens called the "Declaration of Principles." A vote on, and the acceptance of, the "Constitution and By-Laws of the Niagara Movement" closed the first meeting.

Before the Niagara Movement ceased operating, it held four meetings, the second of which occurred in August 1906 at Harper's Ferry. This meeting was distinct because the group paid homage to John Brown, the man who unsuccessfully tried to lead a slave revolt in 1859. Du Bois's remarks were read on the final day of the conference and were the most compelling of the conference. "Address to the Country" included a five-point resolution that demanded quality education, enforcement of the Fourteenth Amendment, and both justice and jobs for African Americans.

Du Bois with other Niagara movement leaders at Harpers Ferry in 1906.

Walling investigated and then chronicled the Springfield riots in his article "Race War in the North" in the September 1908 edition of the *Independent*. The article came out twenty-four hours after the adjournment of the fourth annual Niagara Movement meeting. In the article, Walling accused the North of no longer caring about racial tensions, arguing that the abolitionists and advocates that worked to free the slaves no longer cared. It was a true call to action, and one that Mary Ovington White took to heart. Walling also gathered other progressive friends like Ray Baker, Lillian Wald, Rabbi Stephen Wise, and Oswald Villard to meet and take action. Walling and these associates worked to draft a manifesto for their group. They wanted something dramatic but not too radical. Villard was nominated to draft the document because he owned both the *Evening Post* and the *Nation* and could help the group publish their ideas.

The chairman of the NAACP Executive Committee and one of the NAACP founders, William English Walling.

The group, including Du Bois, began meeting in Villard's apartment regularly. Their goal was to release their manifesto to the public on President Lincoln's birthday, February 12, 1909. Using Lincoln's birthday would be a reminder of Lincoln's ideals, the Emancipation Proclamation, and a direct rebuttal of the Springfield riots. The group of writers began as an all-white group, of which Du Bois was not immediately a part. Then, at Ovington's suggestion, the "Committee on the Status of the Negro" (as it was then called), invited two black clergymen. As the group began to grow, they were forced to find another meeting space outside of Villard's apartment. After almost four meetings, Dr. William L. Bulkley, the only black public school principal in New York City, joined the Committee. From there, Isabel Eaton, who had collaborated with Du Bois on his Philadelphia study, also joined the committee. With the addition of Bulkley and Eaton, the Committee decided that it would launch a biracial campaign to defend and improve the rights of black Americans, and that they would hold a public conference that spring. When the manifesto was released, it included sixty-nine signatures. Eleventh on the list was Du Bois's signature. Booker T. Washington's name was not on the list, and he was not an attendee at the first meeting of the National Negro Conference on May 31, 1909.

The conference had approximately three hundred attendees. Women comprised one third of the attendees. Black attendees were definitely in the minority, but their presence was noticeable. Du Bois, of course, was also an attendee and speaker. He gave a speech entitled "Politics and Industry," which detailed the history of three waves of black disenfranchisement. He fervently argued that until the black man was able to vote, he would not advance economically, nor could he ever be a true ally to white voters and laborers. Opposing the general argument of Washington, Du Bois argued economic power would not come until African Americans gained political power. The NAACP slowly began the process of becoming the organization it is today, and Du Bois wrote and spoke at events for it as it grew.

Off to a Rocky Start

Villard and the resolutions committee drafted final resolutions to be voted on by the whole conference. On June 21, 1909, over one thousand members voted to reprimand the President of the United States, demand strict enforcement of civil rights via the Fourteenth and Fifteenth Amendments, insist on access to the ballot like all other male citizens, and call for equal educational opportunities in all states. The conference attendees agreed on the resolutions, but the organizational structure still needed to be agreed upon.

The real victory of the conference came on July 1. The National Committee for the Advancement of the Negro was voted into existence—the first incarnation of the NAACP. Du Bois was appointed chair of the committee to nominate the interim governing body, which was be called the Committee of Forty. On that day, Du Bois quickly read forty names, and the National Negro Conference came to a close with a whole new organization born. Not everyone was satisfied with the organizational structure, however. The conference wrapped up quickly to prevent any disagreement with the members chosen to be included in the Committee of Forty, or about whether African Americans should be involved in it.

Ida B. Wells-Barnett, Monroe Trotter, and Milton Waldron were three major African-American advocates at the conference who were not included on the official Committee of Forty governing body. Wells-Barnett's exclusion from the list caused quite a bit of drama—the details of which are still unclear. At first, Wells-Barnett blamed both Du Bois and Ovington directly for her omission from the Committee. Another version of Wells-Barnett's omission from the ruling committee is that Du Bois thought she had declined a spot in favor of another advocate. Even if this version is true, Du Bois was not entirely in charge of the Committee of Forty. He likely wielded the most power as a black man in the new organization, but his role was subordinate to Villard's. Despite all the consternation with the initial Committee of Forty, Wells-Barnett went down in history as one of two African-American women who signed the initial call to form the NAACP in 1909, despite being marginalized from future leadership positions in the organization. At its birth, the organization was primarily composed of white members who, somewhat ironically, fought for African-American inclusion in political life.

Du Bois described the creation of the Committee of Forty in the Survey. Despite these disagreements, he chronicled the results of the conference in a euphoric tone. The tone didn't reflect the tension between members, but the article marketed the organization very well. Du Bois wrote:

> So the conference adjourned. Its net result was the vision of future cooperation, not simply as in the past, between giver and beggar—the older ideal of charity—but a new alliance between experienced social workers and reformers in touch on the one hand with scientific philanthropy and on the other with the great struggling mass of laborers of all kinds, whose condition and needs know no color line.

While the initial moments of the NAACP were not without conflict, the conference ended with the creation of a new civil rights organization built on vision, compromise, and racial equality. And with the birth of this new organization, a new phase of Du Bois's life and work also began.

Du Bois Anchors the NAACP

When Du Bois returned to Atlanta, he knew that he would have to decide whether to maintain his life as a scholar or whether he could become a full-time activist working with the National Negro Committee. Working with the organization was difficult, however,

Another founding member of the NAACP, Oswald Villard, resisted African-American involvement in the early days of the organization.

due to tension among its members, and Du Bois was restricted from taking on a larger leadership role. The committee chairman, Oswald Villard, was unreceptive to having more than a few African Americans on the Committee of Forty, so much so that he removed some names of black members from the list. Walling, on the other hand, advocated for more inclusion of African Americans and even successfully had the Committee of Forty extended to become the

Committee of Fifty. Du Bois was on the Committee, of course, and the extension allowed Wells-Barnett back on, among others.

Settling on a ruling committee was a challenge in the early stages. Villard was difficult, but he had wealth and great influence, so he needed to be accommodated. Other leaders, like Walling and Ovington, recognized Villard's influence but also knew that Du Bois was indispensable as an organizer and was greatly supported by all of the other black Committee members. Villard's influence continued to grow while other Committee of Forty members, including Walling, lost some of their power. Meanwhile, Du Bois, who was in Atlanta teaching and working, missed a few crucial committee meetings in early 1910. Although Du Bois was not putting in long hours deciding on leaders and organizational structure, he was at the center of many of the organization's decisions.

Villard disagreed with Walling and Ovington over several issues, including whether or not to permit Du Bois to take on a leadership role in the organization. Then Villard wrote an editorial titled, "Mr. Washington in Politics" for the April 1 edition of the *Evening Post*. In the editorial, Villard challenged the leadership of Booker T. Washington and complimented Du Bois. The title and the content of the editorial paraphrased and paid homage to Du Bois's essay "Of Mr. Booker T. Washington and Others" from *The Souls of Black Folk*. With the editorial, Villard extended an olive branch to Du Bois and gained more support for the organization. Not long after the appearance of the editorial, donations began coming in more steadily. Members were happy that the National Negro Committee's goals were publicized in anticipation of the May 12 national meeting.

Walling, Ovington, and other leaders knew that the survival of the young organization depended on charisma and the support of a critical group of engaged black Americans. For many on the National Committee, this meant more involvement from Du Bois. Walling argued that until they offered a role and a salary to Du Bois, or someone similar, the committee could do little to advance their cause.

Du Bois demonstrated his leadership as he set the theme of the second annual conference in May, 1910: "Disenfranchisement and Its Effects upon the Negro." During the conference, the Preliminary Committee on Organization was also adopted, based on Du Bois's plans. With this adoption, the Committee on the Status of the Negro officially became the National Association for the Advancement of Colored People (NAACP). Colored was chosen as an adjective so as to advocate for individuals with dark skin, not just those who are classified as African American. The success of the conference and the increased publicity of the NAACP solidified Du Bois's future with the organization.

The Official NAACP

The NAACP emerged from the 1910 conference as a new force in the movement for equal rights. Membership was $2 annually, or else a lifetime membership could be purchased for $500, which included a special plaque and free tickets for special events. Moorfield Storey, a lawyer from Boston and a past president of the American Bar Association, was elected as president of the NAACP. Du Bois was considered the prospective director of publicity and research, but there still was no money for his salary. Then, in early June of that year, Walling wrote to Du Bois offering him the position and assuring him that they would eventually raise the funds necessary for his salary.

The *Crisis*

As the director of publicity and research for the NAACP, Du Bois arrived in New York with the idea to start a national monthly magazine called the *Crisis*. Many civil rights publications had failed, and the organizers of the NAACP did not seem optimistic that a new one would find any success. In addition, the organization did not have any funds to contribute to its publication. Regardless, Du Bois wrote up a prospectus calling for five thousand subscribers at one dollar apiece. The function of the publication would be to record global events that greatly affected African Americans, to review opinions and literature related to racial issues, and to serve as a forum for the rights of all irrespective of race. On September 6, 1910, the executive committee approved the *Crisis* as the official publication of the NAACP. At the beginning of November, the first issue officially went on sale at ten cents a copy.

The Crisis was a militant publication in the tradition of Frederick Douglass's *North Star* and William Lloyd Garrison's *Liberator*. Both papers were crucial to the abolition movement prior to the Civil War. Du Bois wanted the *Crisis* to be crucial to the fight for the enfranchisement of blacks. Du Bois's introductory editorial set the tone when he declared that the publication intended to show the dangers of racial prejudice. From the first issue on, the *Crisis* followed the same pattern. The "Along the Color Line" section had articles and subsections related to politics, education, organizations and meetings, and science and art. The "Opinion" section canvassed the press and other correspondents on the issues, while the large "Editorial" section covered the business aspects of the NAACP. Civil, economic, political, and, of course, violent atrocities committed against African Americans were focused on in "The Burden." Sections like "What to Read," "Talks About Women," and "Men of the Month" were added in the next few issues.

Almost immediately, the *Crisis* became a popular periodical that increased support for the NAACP. Due in part to the popularity of this publication, the organization began to grow. Over time, Du Bois exerted his greatest influence on American society as the editor and manager for this politically important and well-received civil rights publication.

COPYRIGHT
1907
J. E. PURDY
BY
BOSTON
NO 1

CHAPTER FIVE

The Great Advocate

L ooking back, it is hard to determine whether Du Bois's writings or his work on behalf of the NAACP had more of an influence on early twentieth-century society. He keenly felt the problem of segregation and the injustice of racial inequality, and he expressed these issues eloquently and rationally. By writing his many articles, essays, and books, Du Bois was able to articulate the arguments that American society needed to hear. In fact, it was his early writings that put him in the national spotlight, and which allowed Du Bois to eventually help found the NAACP.

Early Writings

Whether Du Bois was a student, on faculty at a university, or working on behalf of organizations like the NAACP, he

Du Bois's writings would always challenge readers and advocate for black Americans.

always wrote and published articles about issues affecting African Americans. Du Bois began writing while he was still at Great Barrington High for the *New York Globe*. Between 1883 and 1885, he published a total of twenty-four articles in the *Globe* and its successor, the *Freeman*. He also used his experience and success with the *Globe* to begin writing for the *Springfield Republican*, the largest newspaper in Western Massachusetts, as a special, anonymous correspondent. His pieces generally reported on the black community, and they included uplifting commentary and ideas for political action. Over time, Du Bois's writing became more pointedly a vehicle for racial and social justice.

Although Du Bois was a prolific writer, it wasn't his day job. Du Bois concurrently taught and oftentimes conducted sociological studies, too. In order to write, he had to carefully schedule the spare time he had to meet his writing goals. Even with time constraints, Du Bois managed to publish sixteen books in his lifetime. Du Bois's first published book was his dissertation, *The Suppression of the African Slave-Trade to the United States of America, 1638-1870*. Du Bois's next two publications were sociological studies of African Americans in Atlanta and Philadelphia. These texts were academic in nature and didn't necessarily appeal to the average American, white or black. *The Souls of Black Folk* was a whole different kind of text, and arguably one that wouldn't be matched in its reception and subsequent fame by any other of his books.

Du Bois explained the genesis of the book came from the publisher, McClurg. In 1902, an editor at McClurg asked Du Bois to write and compile several essays to be released as a book. At first, Du Bois was leery of the opportunity because he thought essay collections often fell flat, and did not prove to be all that useful or moving. Eventually, he acquiesced and started compiling the essays that would make up the famous *The Souls of Black Folk*.

The *Suppression* *of the* *African Slave Trade* *in the* *United States* *of America.* 1638–1871 *by* W.E. Burghardt Du Bois, A.M., Professor of Ancient Languages in Wilberforce University. 1895.

The cover of Du Bois's first published book, his dissertation on the African slave trade.

Du Bois vs. Washington

At the turn of the century, many of Du Bois's articles and essays were in conversation with Booker T. Washington and other leaders in the black community. The death of Frederick Douglass in 1895 played a large role in Du Bois's writing. Many leaders of the black community saw Booker T. Washington as the next great African-American leader, and Washington had the support of many white leaders and politicians. Du Bois, however, had a lot of philosophical differences with Washington and over time his writing addressed their differences. Du Bois continually argued for African Americans to have the right to vote, as well as access to economic success and quality education. These arguments often contradicted Washington, who encouraged blacks to be industrious first and foremost. His commentaries and arguments appeared in publications like the *Dial* or the *Atlantic Monthly*.

Washington was not a gifted writer like Du Bois, but his autobiography, *Up From Slavery,* was extremely popular beginning in 1901. In the book, Washington emphasized his successes and, while he did disparage slavery, he did not write of its legacy as a hindrance to his own success. Unlike Du Bois, whose fame in the black community would grow with the publication of *The Souls of Black Folk,* Washington was already quite famous when he published *Up From Slavery.*

One of Washington's most famous speeches, the Atlanta Exposition Address, was incorporated into his autobiography with its famous metaphor of casting down one's bucket. According to Washington, whites should hire blacks, and blacks should seek to be good, hard workers. He urged blacks to work in agriculture, mechanics, and domestic service, especially. One of the fundamental issues that Du Bois disagreed with was Washington's emphasis on manual labor and vocational education. Washington writes, "No race prospers till it learns that there is as much dignity in tilling a field as writing a poem." Du Bois, as a highly educated black man who received many opportunities because of his education, vehemently disagreed with the sentiment. He didn't disagree that there could be dignity in tilling a field, but he didn't believe that a black man should have to till a field if he wanted to pursue education and a different profession instead.

One of the biggest differences between Du Bois and Washington's outlooks on the status of African Americans in the United States was how Du Bois valued the creativity and imagination of the black community. He lauded slaves for their spirituality in the "sorrow songs," which he featured in *The Souls of Black Folk*. He even identified these slave spirituals as the only distinctly American songs at the time. Du Bois recognized imagination as a source of black strength, something that would become a cornerstone of the Harlem Renaissance. By putting much of what he believed about black culture and the imagination in *The Souls of Black Folk*, Du Bois created a book very different from Washington's *Up From Slavery*.

Critical Reception of *The Souls of Black Folk*

In "The Afterthought," the conclusion of *The Souls of Black Folk*, Du Bois stated his fear that the ideas expressed in the text would not reach and engage in the wider world. He was wrong. By June 1903, the book went into its third printing. By the fall of the same year, the text was selling two hundred copies per week and, five years later, nearly ten thousand copies of *The Souls of Black Folk* had been sold in total. In 1905, a British publisher put out an edition and shortly thereafter a German translation of the text was published. The number of copies sold was impressive on its own, but its reception was even more impressive in light of the fact that the book was a controversial text written about African Americans by an African-American man.

The text was not welcomed by all readers, however. Booker T. Washington disagreed with the book in principle. Washington and his supporters, the Tuskegee Machine, as they were called, controlled a large number of African-American presses, and those publications did not review *The Souls of Black Folk*. Washington and his influence stopped the reviews from being written. Similarly, the majority of white Southern newspapers ignored *The Souls of Black Folk*. When the book was reviewed, the reviewer generally claimed he didn't know what to make of it. There were also more extreme reactions to the text, as well. A reviewer for the *Nashville American* called the book dangerous for black Americans to read. One of the most extreme reactions to the text was published in the *Houston Chronicle,* when the reviewer demanded that Du Bois be indicted for inciting rape.

Outside the South, not all of the reviews were extremely positive, either. Even in the North, to review Du Bois's book and admit that it was well-written and persuasive would go against the status quo. The *New York Times* had a white Southerner write an anonymous review of the book. The reviewer conceded that *The Souls of Black Folk* was a text worth considering but thought that Du Bois, as a Northerner, only had a superficial understanding of black Southerners.

The Souls of Black Folks had a profound influence on more than just black and white residents of the United States. For example, a young Russian immigrant strongly identified with Du Bois's words and wrote him a letter praising his work and opening his eyes to the inequities that African Americans faced. As additional printings, and translations, of the text went into circulation, Du Bois's double consciousness spoke to readers from a variety of racial, religious, national, and socio-economic backgrounds.

Many of Du Bois's contemporaries praised *The Soul of Black Folk*, as well. Ida B. Wells-Barnett had a lively debate about the text at a literary gathering in Chicago. The result of the debate led a Unitarian minister who was in attendance to declare that she wanted to devote her life to helping African Americas. Jessie Fauset, who would one day become a writer of the Harlem Renaissance and who would also work closely with Du Bois, was an undergraduate at Cornell University. Fauset wrote and thanked Du Bois for writing *The Souls of Black Folk.* A review in the *Ohio Entertainer* implored every person, whether white or black, to read and study the book. An anonymous review that appeared in the *Nation* noted that anyone who thought that Du Bois, while extremely smart and intellectual, was a bit cold, would be pleasantly surprised by the warmth of the text and its depth.

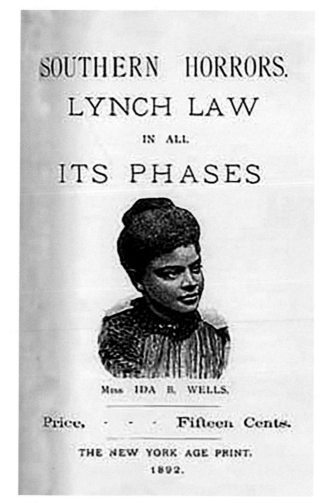

An advocate of *The Souls of Black Folk*, Wells-Barnett wrote often on the evils of lynching.

Du Bois's Lifelong Principles

History frames many of Du Bois's works as direct responses to Booker T. Washington's ideas, but Du Bois had strong beliefs and ideas that were articulated for other reasons than to refute Washington. In 1906, he addressed the Niagara Conference and declared the need for equal rights. He famously stated, "We will

" C R E D O "

On the anniversary of his son's death, October 2, 1904, Du Bois wrote his own credo, or set of beliefs. The resulting prose poem, "Credo," is a political manifesto and declaration of racial pride. It was published on October 6, 1904. "Credo" reads like a religious creed, something that reinforces belief and gives readers a great insight into what Du Bois believed about human beings and racial equality.

Toward the end of "Credo," Du Bois writes: "I believe in Liberty for all men; the space to stretch their arms and their souls. The right to breathe and the right to vote, the freedom to choose their friends, enjoy the sunshine, and ride the railroads, uncursed by color: thinking, dreaming, working so they will in a kingdom of Beauty and Love."

not be satisfied to take one jot or tittle less than our full manhood rights." His conference address also enumerated the rights that he and the black community were demanding, beginning with the right to vote. Du Bois, who never saw a dramatic improvement in voting rights for the black community in his life, always advocated for the right to vote, first and foremost.

Du Bois recognized that, although slavery was no longer legal, the South and much of the United States had employed a new form of slavery through segregation and the Jim Crow laws. He constantly referred back to this idea as he wrote *The Souls of Black Folk,* and he would continue to return to this theme in future writings and speeches. Although a black person could no longer be legally enslaved, there were so many codes and rules restricting their political rights that their freedom was almost nonexistent. As Du Bois wrote his essays, he didn't envision a promised land for African Americans after slavery. Instead, he believed that African Americans had moved from simple bondage (slavery) to more complex bondage (segregation and Jim Crow). As an activist in the Niagara Movement and the NAACP, Du Bois worked hard to eliminate this complex bondage for people of color.

Success for the *Crisis* and Du Bois

Although *The Souls of Black Folk* made Du Bois a prominent thought leader of the early civil rights movement, Du Bois remained on the faculty of Atlanta University. For many years, Du Bois felt that his greatest duty was to remain a scholar in Atlanta. However, that changed with the founding of the NAACP. It was not until June 1910 that he was formally offered a position with the NAACP, and it was certainly a financial risk for Du Bois to accept the position, as the organization did not yet have guaranteed funds to pay his salary. However, Atlanta University was continually losing funds to Tuskegee, funds that Du Bois could have used in his academic pursuits. So Du Bois looked at the opportunity with the NAACP as

Standing in the back row, Du Bois posed with the rest of the faculty and staff at Atlanta University in 1906.

a fork in the road and chose to confront the problem of the twentieth century—segregation—as an activist instead of a scholar.

As soon as the NAACP formally employed Du Bois, he helped found and begin the *Crisis*—the NAACP's monthly magazine. Du Bois set the tone with an introductory editorial in which he declared that the magazine would show the danger of race prejudice, and then dove into articles on lynching and other racial atrocities. From that first issue onward, Du Bois never failed to expose or criticize institutions or situations that he felt needed closer examination. For example, in May 1912, he criticized the African-American Christian church—an institution that was seldom criticized from within the black community. In the editorial, he acknowledged the positive works of the church, especially during slavery, but went on to call it out for dishonest leadership. Du Bois did not shy away from criticizing predominantly African-American institutions.

Under Du Bois's leadership, the *Crisis* didn't shy away from any controversial subjects, either—even the subject of interracial marriage. In many states, interracial marriage was illegal. Du Bois took on this topic in the September 1911 issue with the lead editorial titled "Social Equality." While he stated that interracial marriage wasn't necessarily discussed among the black community nor necessarily thought of, he argued that the right to marry whoever one chooses, regardless of race, must be defended. This editorial shocked its black readers as much as its white ones.

As Du Bois was hitting his stride as editor of the *Crisis*, he achieved another one of his goals—publishing a novel. In October 1911, *The Quest of the Silver Fleece* was published. Du Bois had worked on the novel on and off for over five years. It was published even after severe criticisms about its language, style, and the second half of the text being much less interesting. The novel itself was loosely based on a classical myth, and the plot weaves together black and white lives in the rural South, Washington, DC, and New York. The novel would never be considered the great work that *The Souls of Black Folk* was, but it demonstrated his growing popularity.

THE CRISIS

A RECORD OF THE DARKER RACES

Volume One   NOVEMBER, 1910   Number One

Edited by W. E. BURGHARDT DU BOIS, with the co-operation of Oswald Garrison Villard, J. Max Barber, Charles Edward Russell, Kelly Miller, W. S. Braithwaite and M. D. Maclean.

CONTENTS

Along the Color Line   3

Opinion   7

Editorial   10

The N. A. A. C. P.   12

Athens and Brownsville   13
By MOORFIELD STOREY

The Burden   14

What to Read . . .   15

PUBLISHED MONTHLY BY THE

National Association for the Advancement of Colored People

AT TWENTY VESEY STREET   NEW YORK CITY

ONE DOLLAR A YEAR   TEN CENTS A COPY

The inaugural issue of the *Crisis* in 1910.

The *Crisis,* which still exists as a publication today, was extremely popular in its first decade of circulation, thanks in a large part to Du Bois. In January 1911, the *Crisis* sold 3,000 issues. Its readership continued to grow over the next several months, with 4,000 copies sold in February and 6,000 in March. Historically black colleges and universities, like Atlanta and Fisk, began supporting the magazine. New features were added to later issues such as "Earning a Living," which looked at the groundbreaking achievements of black surgeons, psychiatrists, inventors, and other professionals worthy of emulation. In April 1912, circulation reached 22,500 readers and, by 1914, the magazine reached 33,000 subscribers. In December 1917, the *Crisis* famously sold over fifty thousand issues—53,750 to be exact. With the success of the *Crisis,* Du Bois was finally granted a $3,600 annual salary by the board. For many readers, it was Du Bois himself who defined the NAACP through his work at the *Crisis.*

Du Bois's personality made the *Crisis* a unique, successful publication. Although Du Bois was not religious, his writing about race, politics, and the pursuit of democracy and justice contained such fervor that it was practically a religion in and of itself. Readers were often moved by the passion with which Du Bois wrote and, in this way, they were also forced to face prejudices they might not otherwise have had to face. One example of this was when Du Bois forced the issue of African-American female membership in the National American Woman **Suffrage** Association as women fought for the right to vote prior to 1920. This was not a popular position at the time, but Du Bois expertly expressed the importance of including African-American women in the fight for women's voting rights. the *Crisis* was also very influential in the 1912 presidential election. During the campaign, the magazine was full of advertisements placed by Republican, Democratic, and Progressive parties, although most of these political parties only did so because it reached so many readers.

The circulation of the *Crisis* peaked at 100,000 and averaged around 60,000 a month in the early 1920s. Even though readership wasn't growing by this point, it was the premier civil rights publication by and for people of color. Some criticized the *Crisis* as predictable and even prickly in its political opinions, but even detractors acknowledged that it was a journal with a courageous editor.

While the *Crisis* may not have been growing in popularity, it began to play more of a role as a literary magazine. Jessie Fauset worked as the literary editor from 1919 to 1926 and, under her direction, the *Crisis* sponsored short story and other fiction competitions. Langston Hughes's first published poem, "The Negro Speaks Rivers," appeared first in the *Crisis*. The June 1923 issue announced the results of its Prize Story Competition and also ran the poem "Bread and Wine" by a young, black poet named Countee Cullen. the *Crisis* played a profound role in publishing the works of writers of the Harlem Renaissance—even before it became known as such—as it remained focused on political and civil rights for black Americans.

Literary editor of the *Crisis*, Jessie Redmon Fauset, also had a personal relationship with Du Bois.

Du Bois, indirectly, helped spark creation in the Harlem Renaissance movement. In a *Crisis* editorial titled "Art For Nothing," Du Bois urged the black community to support African-American artists such as himself, with the publication of his novel. Du Bois, along with writers like Alain Locke, James Weldon Johnson and Jessie Fauset, believed another way to combat racism was through artistic work and discipline. Art had the possibility to transform the negative images of the black community that a majority of white Americans held. The May 1923 issue of the *Crisis* included "The Debut of the Younger School of Negro Writers." This feature inspired editors at the *Opportunity*, a competing publication more focused on social sciences and education, to make it a literary and artistic publication. By 1924, the *Crisis* was sponsoring a series of literary and artistic prizes and, in 1925, Du Bois wrote in the *Crisis* that Alain Locke's *The New Negro* was an extraordinary book that would serve as an **epoch** for literary creation in that time. Du Bois had to praise Locke's anthology because his introductory essay to the collection paid homage to Du Bois and *The Souls of Black Folk*. In the essay, Locke acknowledged Du Bois's double consciousness and then encouraged the creation of a distinctly black expression in art and literature.

Struggles

While working as editor of the *Crisis,* Du Bois also had other ideas for publications and projects. Oftentimes, the NAACP leadership wanted him to focus solely on the civil rights organization and their publication. One semisuccessful project that Du Bois took on was a magazine devoted to young African Americans called the *Brownies' Book.* The magazine came from Du Bois's own experience reading textbooks that only explained white history and included nothing about African Americans. The magazine only ran twenty-four issues from January 1920 through December 1921, most likely due to financing, although it did receive many letters from young readers who loved it. Although the *Brownies' Book* didn't have longevity, it allowed Du Bois to raise the issue of **multicultural education** among his readership.

As time went on, Du Bois struggled with the internal disagreements that had plagued the NAACP since its foundation. As the Harlem Renaissance progressed, Du Bois—despite his own love and admiration for literature—argued that the NAACP was focusing too much on art and literature and too little on a political agenda.

Langston Hughes, one of the most prominent voices in the Harlem Renaissance, as photographed by Carl Van Vechten.

Many members found Du Bois difficult to work with. At other times, the NAACP's board would try to cut back on Du Bois's power with *The Crisis*. Sometimes Du Bois would threaten to resign altogether from both the NAACP and the *Crisis*—which he eventually did in 1934 over the question of whether or not the NAACP should advocate for integration. Du Bois's views on race and equality continued to evolve and caused much disagreement between him and the directors of the NAACP. He eventually was fired from the organization in 1948.

Great Achievements

In June 1920, the NAACP made a bold statement as it selected Atlanta as the site for its eleventh annual conference. The organization had never held a national meeting in the Deep South, and the Atlanta branch of the NAACP had just been organized in 1919. By holding the meeting there, the NAACP demanded that residents of Atlanta and the South take notice of the NAACP's growth and its opposition to Jim Crow. Du Bois was part of the decision and encouraged the board of directors to set the meeting in Atlanta. He also included an editorial in the May issue of the *Crisis* in which he declared that African-American citizens demanded full rights in the South as well as everywhere else.

Although Jim Crow rules were stronger than ever in Atlanta, the mayor and the Chamber of Commerce of Atlanta did invite the organization to hold their annual conference in the city. By 1920, the NAACP was growing, and it was advantageous to maintain a good relationship with the organization. The city's acquiescence was partly an apology for the Atlanta riot in 1906. The invitation was also likely a way of asserting that segregation and civil rights could coexist. However, there was a laundry list of civil rights issues in the South that the NAACP was deeply concerned about. In Lexington, Kentucky, a gun battle killed five black men and led to the lynching of another black man. The state of Mississippi had banned the circulation of any materials or publications that favored or advocated for social equality. And, after being beaten in Texas, the NAACP's executive secretary (who was white), decided to resign. With all the turmoil in the South, it was more important than ever that an organization like the NAACP fought for the rights of African Americans.

The conference also brought Du Bois an honor that underscored how important his thoughts, writing, and organizing were to the NAACP and the struggle for civil rights on behalf of African Americans. Bishop John Hurst, the chairman for the selection committee, presented Du Bois with the Spingarn Medal as a symbol that both Du Bois and his magazine, the *Crisis*, were the NAACP's greatest assets. At the age of fifty-two, Du Bois was acknowledged for his scholarly and literary work, as well as for being instrumental to laying the foundation for equal rights for people of color. After receiving the prestigious Spingarn Medal at age fifty-two, he still felt there was plenty of work to do, but his reputation was without equal worldwide. Even in Europe, Du Bois was regarded as the most important African-American thinker.

To black Americans who knew and followed the work of Du Bois, there was no one else with his intellect and principles—and the award reflected that reality. Earlier in 1920, he had published his seventh book, *Darkwater: Voices from Within the Veil,* which included a semiautobiography with essays and social commentary. The reception of *Darkwater* was much different than *The Souls of Black Folk*. Many of the reviews were harsh. In many cases, the book was written off as an angry invective caused by racial hatred. However, the black community was extremely proud of the book. The reception of *Darkwater* solidified that fact that Du Bois was considered the undisputed "leader" of the civil rights movement. Its book sales matched those of *The Souls of Black Folk* in its first ten years, selling nearly ten thousand copies. The difference, however, was that Southern farmers, sharecroppers, and average African Americans bought the book this time. Du Bois's autobiography wasn't too cerebral and academic—and it reached the average person. It was becoming apparent that Du Bois wasn't just a thought leader for NAACP activists and wealthy philanthropists, but also for the average African-American citizen.

CHAPTER SIX

⌒

W. E. B. Du Bois and the NAACP Today

The general understanding today is that African Americans founded the NAACP, because it continues to work as an advocacy organization primarily for black Americans. Du Bois was involved in the founding of the organization, but it was not founded completely by black Americans. Mary White Ovington and the millionaire William Walling were the true architects of the organization, with Charles Edward Russell and Oswald Villard serving as the organizing engines—and they were all white. Du Bois, however, was in conversation with the major founders and worked diligently to get the organization off the ground—even when he had disagreements, oftentimes with Villard. As part of the founding of the organization, Du Bois chronicled many of the organization's early actions. In a keen public relations move, he exaggerated the contributions of the black community as he

{ Du Bois in 1945 as a delegate to the Pan-African Conference.

summarized the founding of the NAACP for various publications. In Du Bois's version of the founding, the black community was deeply involved.

Du Bois was still on faculty at Atlanta University and working with limited funds during the formative months of the NAACP. He was unable to travel to New York as he would have liked to do during its formative months, and he did not have the connections others, like Walling or Villard, had in order to gain supporters for the organization. Du Bois was not one of the main organizers of the NAACP. On the other hand, Du Bois's books, articles, lectures, letters, and personality all contributed to the formation of the organization. He had been strongly involved in earlier versions of the organization, particularly the Niagara Movement, as well. His power of persuasion encouraged the formation of an organization when many whites were ready to say that nothing could be done. Other organizers, like Ovington and Walling, knew that the organization wouldn't survive without steady involvement from Du Bois.

NAACP Takes On a Life of Its Own

While Du Bois formally worked on public relations and tirelessly edited and wrote for the *Crisis*, the NAACP began to find its identity as an advocacy organization. In the early years, the NAACP was based in New York City where it was originally founded after the Springfield riots. Early on, the organization established branch offices in cities like Boston, Baltimore, Kansas City, Washington, DC, Detroit, and St. Louis. Meanwhile, NAACP membership began picking up steam. In 1917, the organization had around nine thousand members and, by 1919, it boasted ninety thousand members. There were also three hundred local branches—the NAACP had taken hold in more than just the major cities. There was a lot of optimism at this time, as the Harlem Renaissance was beginning to take off and writer and diplomat James Weldon Johnson became the NAACP's first black secretary in 1920. During

Du Bois stands front and center with the Junior Auxiliary NAACP Delegates in 1929 in Cleveland, Ohio.

this time, Du Bois influenced both the NAACP and the artistic movement of the Harlem Renaissance with his writing.

The early years of the NAACP helped the organization establish itself as a legal advocate for people of color. Two major incidents helped solidify the organization in its very early years. The NAACP helped advocate against a discriminatory Oklahoma law that regulated voting through a grandfather clause. The 1910 case, *Guinn v. United States*, was a victory for the NAACP. The new organization also used publicity, with Du Bois and the *Crisis*, to fight against and boycott the release of the 1915 film *A Birth of a Nation*.

D.W. Griffith's film was criticized by the organization then, and still today, for the demeaning and inflammatory stereotypes of African Americans and its glorification of the **Ku Klux Klan**.

One of the most crucial issues for the black community at the time was lynching. The NAACP made stopping the practice of lynching one of their top priorities in the early years. The organization supported and advocated the passing of the federal Dyer Bill. The Dyer Bill, if it were made law, would have punished participants and those who failed to prosecute lynch mobs. The bill successfully passed the US House of Representatives in 1922 but it would never pass the Senate. In fact, a bill would never be passed outlawing lynching in the United States. The NAACP continued to research and demanded an end to lynching with the new president, Walter White, at the helm of the NAACP. White was a very fair-skinned African American and was able to infiltrate white groups and gather more information on the atrocities of lynching. In addition to his anti-lynching work, White was able to successfully block the segregationist judge John Parker's nomination to the US Supreme Court bench by President Herbert Hoover. Because so many legal issues were decided at the Supreme Court level, blocking a judge that was prosegregation was a major victory for the NAACP.

It was during the 1930s and White's tenure as president that the NAACP settled into its role as a legal advocate. In 1930, the NAACP commissioned the Margold Report to create a legal plan to attack segregation. Segregation was legalized in 1896 with *Plessy v. Ferguson*. The report planned to attack the "separate but equal" doctrine and the inherent illegality of segregation through the public school system. The campaign began with lawsuits for equal facilities for graduate and professional schools. In 1935, Charles H. Houston, Howard University's law school dean, became the NAACP's chief counsel. His school-segregation legal battles paved the way for the 1954 ruling in *Brown v. Board of Education*, which finally outlawed segregation.

Eleanor Roosevelt, first lady, also served as an NAACP board member.

During the Great Depression and the 1930s, African Americans were disproportionately struggling. At that time, the NAACP turned its focus to economic justice and worked closely with labor unions, specifically the Congress of Industrial Organizations. White spent a lot of time meeting with Eleanor Roosevelt, an NAACP board member and the wife of President Franklin D. Roosevelt, to convince the president to outlaw job discrimination based on race in the armed forces, defense industries, and agencies started by Roosevelt's **New Deal**. Ultimately, Roosevelt opened thousands of jobs to African Americans after labor leaders, in collaboration with the NAACP, threatened a national March on Washington in 1941. This idea would serve as inspiration for the historical 1963 March on Washington. Roosevelt also enacted the Fair Employment Practices Committee (FEPC) to ensure compliance.

By the 1940s, the NAACP was truly a national organization with 893 branches. In 1946, the NAACP recorded approximately 600,000 members. As the organization grew, it also became more stable. Because members were loyal, the organization was able to multiply its income and its staff members. As they gained more staff, committees—like the Legal Committee—could dedicate more resources to fighting illegal discrimination and establishing the Legal Defense Fund. Today, the membership of the NAACP is 500,000, and it is headquartered in Baltimore, Maryland.

Legal Victories That Affect Us Today

The NAACP stepped in and advocated on behalf of black citizens who did not have the power to advocate for themselves. In 1917, the NAACP won an important Supreme Court case. The city of Louisville, Kentucky, had enacted an ordinance that required blacks to live only in certain sections of the city. The Court ruled that the ordinance violated the Fourteenth Amendment of the Constitution, which states that all people are entitled to equal protection under the law. In 1923, the NAACP won another case in front of the Supreme Court. This victory guaranteed that blacks could not be excluded from juries.

One of the most famous legal victories for the NAACP came from Charles Hamilton Houston and Thurgood Marshall's hard work. Using Nathan Margold's report, Houston took on the "separate but equal" doctrine in the 1896 *Plessy v. Ferguson* case. Beginning in 1935, Houston employed his "equalization strategy,"

WWW.NAACP.ORG

NAACP

NAACP MISSION

Here is today's NAACP's mission statement as posted on their website:

The mission of the National Association for the Advancement of Colored People is to ensure the political, educational, social, and economic equality of rights of all persons and to eliminate race-based discrimination.

Vision Statement

The vision of the National Association for the Advancement of Colored People is to ensure a society in which all individuals have equal rights without discrimination based on race.

Objectives

The following statement of objectives is found on the first page of the NAACP Constitution. The principal objectives of the Association shall be:

- To ensure the political, educational, social, and economic equality of all citizens
- To achieve equality of rights and eliminate race prejudice among the citizens of the United States
- To remove all barriers of racial discrimination through democratic processes
- To seek enactment and enforcement of federal, state, and local laws securing civil rights
- To inform the public of the adverse effects of racial discrimination and to seek its elimination
- To educate persons as to their constitutional rights and to take all lawful action to secure the exercise thereof, and to take any other lawful action in furtherance of these objectives, consistent with the NAACP's Articles of Incorporation and this Constitution.

W. E. B. Du Bois and the NAACP Today

which included filing lawsuits demanding that school facilities provided for black students be equal to those available for white students. In the beginning, the NAACP did not directly challenge *Plessy v. Ferguson*. Instead, Houston guessed that states that practiced segregation were unable to pay to maintain quality schools for black students. From 1935 to 1940, Houston successfully argued a series of cases with the equalization strategy. *Murray v. Maryland* resulted in the desegregation of the University of Maryland's Law School in 1936. In another similar case, *State ex rel. Gaines v. Canada*, the US Supreme Court ordered that a black student be admitted to the University of Missouri Law School in 1938.

Thurgood Marshall succeeded Houston as the NAACP counsel and continued his equalization strategy campaign. Many of Marshall's cases successfully challenged other facets of segregation. In the mid-1940s, in the case *Smith v. Allwright*, Marshall fought and won against "white primaries" that disallowed African Americans from voting in several southern states. *Shelley v. Kraemer* in 1948 ended the enforcement of racially restrictive covenants that barred blacks from purchasing homes in white neighborhoods. The year 1950 saw laws struck down in both Texas and Oklahoma that required segregated graduate schools in *Sweatt v. Painter* and *McLaurin v. Oklahoma*. In both rulings, the unanimous Supreme Court pointed to the Equal Protection Clause of the Fourteenth Amendment as the reason those states had to admit black students into their graduate and professional schools.

All of the NAACP-supported victories by Houston and then Marshall helped set legal precedent and paved the way for the 1954 *Brown v. Board of Education of Topeka, Kansas* victory. The *Brown* case actually combined six separate cases from five different jurisdictions including Kansas, South Carolina, Virginia, Washington DC, and Delaware. The case was called "Brown" because Oliver Brown was one of many plaintiffs in the Kansas case, and his name appeared first in the list of plaintiffs on the court filings. His specific attorney was Robert Carter, whose innovative strategy was to use the testimony of social

Thurgood Marshall, lawyer for the NAACP, addresses the press after the 1958 landmark *Brown v. Board of Education* verdict.

scientists and other experts. These experts were called on to demonstrate the harm and psychological injuries that segregation caused on African-American students. In the historic decision, the Supreme Court ruled that segregation in public education was a violation of the Equal Protection Clause of the Fourteenth Amendment.

The success of the *Brown v. Board of Education* ruling inspired many more actions in the civil rights movement. Demonstrations in the 1950s and 1960s eventually led to the Civil Rights Act of 1964, the Voting Rights Act of 1965, and the Fair Housing Act of 1968. The NAACP wasn't the organizing arm of the majority of the protests and demonstrations, although they did help coordinate the March on Washington. Instead, the NAACP continued representing civil rights workers and brought various lawsuits as a way to implement the *Brown* ruling in multiple desegregation cases around the country. Additional cases were filed that successfully fought discrimination in public accommodations, housing, employment, and voting.

Today, the NAACP's Legal Department and its attorneys still challenge racial discrimination. Many of their lawsuits are similar to those started back in the 1930s and related to voting disenfranchisement. Others are much different, such as lawsuits to remove state-sponsored symbols of white supremacy, like the Confederate flag. The legal department also focuses on **class actions** in broad areas like employment, education, housing, and criminal law.

NAACP Today

Currently, Cornell William Brooks serves as the eighteenth national executive of the NAACP. Confirmed by the board of directors in May 2014, Brooks was a civil rights attorney, social justice advocate, fourth generation ordained minister and coalition-builder. As the CEO, he works with Association leadership and membership to build an NAACP that is multiracial, multiethnic, multigenerational, and one million members strong. The NAACP's twenty-first-century goals are focused on disparities in access to health care, education, voting, and the criminal justice system. They also to continue to serve as legal advocates.

Today, the NAACP is part of the national conversation on racial justice in America in a way that most engaged citizens accept without question. It is active online and on Twitter through their Twitter handle, @NAACP. When an issue involving racial injustice happens today in the United States, it is expected that the NAACP will make a statement and get involved in the issue.

In 2015, the 106th NAACP annual meeting was held in Philadelphia. In honor of the milestone, Philadelphia journalist Harold Jackson interviewed David Levering Lewis, the premier Du Bois biographer. The article, "The Legacy of W. E. B. Du Bois and the NAACP," included Lewis's reflection on the past, present, and future of the NAACP. Lewis conjectured that Du Bois might be disappointed in today's NAACP—he might have wanted to see the organization taking a greater leadership role in the face of racial injustices.

Du Bois's Legacy

Once Du Bois began working in public relations and editing the *Crisis* on behalf of the NAACP, his views and ideas challenged the organization. Du Bois would often find himself at odds with the board of directors and would have a hard time separating himself from the *Crisis*. As he welcomed the Harlem Renaissance and its artistic expression, he had a hard time welcoming art that wasn't explicitly political. Today, we look back on his essay "Criteria of Negro Art" as representative of his support of the artistic rebirth, when Du Bois himself was rather conflicted about its legacy.

It is important to note, however, that Du Bois once was fired from the NAACP and, another time, he resigned because his new opinions differed from the organization's own stance. Du Bois came full circle on his views regarding segregation. Toward the end of his life, he lost faith in being able to build a uniquely African-American community. Although he applauded (and was shocked by) the 1954 *Brown v. Board of Education* Supreme Court decision that ended legal segregation, he had evolved in his views and saw the value in segregated communities in a way he did not when he wrote *The Souls of Black Folk*. In fact, he came to believe that African-American culture should be preserved, and African Americans should not assimilate with white culture. Over the years, Du Bois also became increasingly involved in pan-Africa conferences and back-to-Africa movements.

With today's technology, nearly all of Du Bois's writings are accessible. Perhaps that is why Du Bois is remembered for coining the term "double consciousness" and not for having been tried as a possible foreign agent by the United States government. Today, Du Bois's concept of double consciousness is still applicable to the struggle of many in the black community to be treated fairly. Many American literature classes place *The Souls of Black Folk* on their syllabi, with special attention paid to the first chapter "Of Our Spiritual Strivings." James Weldon Johnson, author of *The Autobiography of the Ex-Colored Man* and one-time president of the NAACP, declared that Du Bois's *The Souls of Black Folk* had the greatest effect on African Americans since the publication of Harriet Beecher Stowe's *Uncle Tom's Cabin*. While Du Bois is firmly ensconced in American literature, his works assisted in creating a distinctly African-American literature and paved the way for multicultural studies at universities beginning in the 1960s. Many of Du Bois's ideas about double consciousness and the veil would be explored by writers like Countee Cullen, Zora Neale Hurston, Ralph Ellison, and even contemporary writer Zadie Smith.

Finding Du Bois Today

The *Crisis*, one of Du Bois's enduring legacies, continues to be published today, although it is not the direct mouthpiece of the NAACP anymore. It is published quarterly, instead of bi-monthly, but it is still dedicated to serving as a forum for discussing issues confronting people of color as well as American society and the world in general. The magazine includes interviews as well as in-depth reporting. The special section "The NAACP Today" reports on the news and events of the NAACP on both a local and national level.

Today, the W. E. B. Du Bois archives are housed at the University of Massachusetts-Amherst. The archive includes over 100,000 pieces

A modern snapshot of the W. E. B. Du Bois library at the University of Massachusetts–Amherst.

of correspondence, speeches, articles, columns, and manuscripts among audiotapes, photographs, and lots of miscellaneous materials. Much of the material is even accessible online for anyone to examine. *Slate*, an online magazine, recently discussed a newly discovered Du Bois short story called "The Princess Steel." Du Bois, his life, and his writings are still of interest to contemporary Americans.

Although Du Bois's views changed and evolved over his life, today his legacy lies with the work he did early in the twentieth century. The activism that the NAACP did in Du Bois's life and the work it continues to do today is a clear, enduring statement on this great American thinker's relevancy both in his lifetime and today.

CHRONOLOGY

1868 William Edward Burghardt Du Bois is born on February 23. The Fourteenth Amendment is ratified.

1870 The Fifteenth Amendment is enacted.

1884 Du Bois graduates from Great Barrington High School.

1888 After receiving his BA from Fisk University, Du Bois enrolls at Harvard.

1894 Du Bois receives the position of teaching chair in the classics department at Wilberforce University.

1895 Du Bois completes his dissertation and is the first black American to receive a PhD from Harvard University. Booker T. Washington delivers his "Atlanta Exposition Address."

1896 Nina Gomer, a student at Wilberforce, and Du Bois marry. The *Plessy v. Ferguson* ruling makes segregation legal.

1897 Du Bois joins other black intellectuals to found the American Negro Academy, an association dedicated to black scholarly achievement. Du Bois is also appointed professor of history and economics at Atlanta University.

1900 In July, Du Bois attends the first Pan-African Congress in London, is elected secretary, and, in his address, declares segregation to be the biggest problem of the twentieth century.

1901 Booker T. Washington publishes *Up From Slavery*.

1902 Booker T. Washington offers Du Bois a position at Tuskegee University, which he declines.

1903 *The Souls of Black Folk* is published in April.

1905 Du Bois attends the first conference of the Niagara Movement and is elected general secretary.

1906 The Niagara Movement's second meeting is held. Atlanta has historic riots and Du Bois composes his most famous poem, "A Litany of Atlanta."

1908 The final conference of the Niagara Movement is held with few attendees. The Springfield race riot occurs in August.

1909 The National Negro Committee (soon to be the NAACP), made up of mainly whites, is formed, which Du Bois shortly joins.

1910 The NAACP appoints Du Bois as director of publications and research; he then founds the official publication of the NAACP, *The Crisis*. Du Bois is the only black man elected to the board of directors.

1911 The first of Du Bois's novels, *The Quest of the Silver Fleece*, is published.

1914 Du Bois publically supports women's suffrage in the *Crisis*.

1915 Booker T. Washington dies on November 14.

1919 Du Bois writes his famous editorial "Returning Soldiers," which sells the most copies ever for *The Crisis*. He organizes the Pan-African Congress in Paris.

1920 Du Bois's *Darkwater: Voices from Within the Veil* is published.

1922 Du Bois works for the passage of the Dyer Anti-Lynching Bill, which is blocked by the Senate.

1923 Responding to Marcus Garvey, Du Bois writes an article entitled "Back to Africa."

1925 Du Bois contributes "The Negro Mind Reaches Out" to Alain Locke's *The New Negro*.

1926 Du Bois founds the Krigwa Players, a Harlem theater group.

1929 The stock market crashes, thus ushering in the Great Depression.

1930 Howard University awards Du Bois an honorary Doctor of Law degree.

1933 Du Bois relinquishes his editorship of the *Crisis*.

1934 Du Bois grows disillusioned with integration and writes editorials encouraging voluntary segregation. He resigns from the *Crisis* and the NAACP.

1935 The Harlem race riot erupts.

1938 Both Atlanta University and Fisk University award Du Bois with honorary degrees.

1940 Du Bois publishes his autobiography, *Dusk of Dawn*.

1944 The NAACP offers Du Bois a position as director of special research—he accepts and works with Walter White.

1945 Du Bois writes a weekly column for the Chicago *Defender*. He also resigns from the American Association of University Professors to protest their conferences held in segregated hotels.

1954 The Supreme Court outlaws public school segregation in *Brown v. Board of Education of Topeka, Kansas*.

1955 Rosa Parks refuses to give up her seat on a bus in Montgomery, Alabama.

1956 Martin Luther King Jr. organizes the Montgomery bus boycott.

1963 Du Bois becomes a citizen of Ghana. He dies on the eve of the civil rights March on Washington.

GLOSSARY

abolition The movement to end slavery.

accommodationist The ceding of rights to whites to keep the status quo and gain rights later on.

antebellum The time period prior to the Civil War.

assassination The murder of a prominent person.

black nationalist A person who supports a racial definition for national identity.

Communism A social, political, and economic ideology with the goal of common ownership.

Congregationalist A system of church governance in which each church runs its own affairs.

discrimination Unfairly treating a group of people differently from other people and/or groups.

disenfranchise To prevent from having the right to vote.

double consciousness A term coined by Du Bois to describe one's identity as having multiple facets.

feminism The belief that men and women should have equal rights and opportunities.

Freedmen's Bureau A government agency established by Congress in 1865 to assist newly freed blacks and poor whites in the South.

grandfather clause A requirement established in the Jim Crow South to disenfranchise blacks—if your grandfather couldn't vote then you cannot vote.

impeach To charge a public official (while in office) with a crime.

industrialist Someone who owns or manages an industry.

Jim Crow laws Discrimination against blacks by legal enforcement, especially to keep different races separate through segregation.

Ku Klux Klan A post-American Civil War secret society advocating white supremacy.

lynching To kill someone illegally as a punishment for a crime.

multicultural education Education or teaching that incorporates histories, values, beliefs, and texts from people with different cultural backgrounds.

New Deal President Roosevelt's programs during the Great Depression to help give people jobs again.

postbellum The time period after the Civil War.

racism The poor treatment or violence against people of a different race.

ratified The act of being made official by signing or voting.

Reconstruction The period from the end of the Civil War to 1877 in which conditions were set for the South to rejoin the United States.

riot A situation where a large group of people behave in a violent and uncontrolled way.

seceded To withdraw from.

segregation The practice and policy of keeping people of different races, religions, or nationalities separate.

sharecropper A farmer who raises crops on the owner's land.

sit-in A protest where individuals refuse to leave, or stay in place, until they are given their demands.

Socialist A person who advocates socialism—where major industries are owned and controlled by the government.

suffrage The right to vote.

Talented Tenth A term coined by Du Bois to refer to the most talented and educated 10 percent of African Americans.

veto To reject or not approve.

vigilante A person who tries to seek and punish criminals but is not an officer of the law.

vocational Related to special skills and training; generally more applicable to technical and manual labor jobs.

white supremacy The belief that someone who is white is better than all other races and should have control over all other races.

SOURCES

CHAPTER ONE

pg. 9: Takaki, Ronald. *A Different Mirror.* (New York, NY: Back Bay Books, 1993), p. 107.

pg. 14: Levering Lewis, David. *W.E.B. Du Bois Biography of a Race.* (New York, New York: Henry Holt, 1993) p. 17.

pg. 16: Du Bois, W.E.B. *The Autobiography of W. E. B. Du Bois: A Soliloquy on Viewing My Life from the Last Decade of Its First Century.* (New York, New York: International Publishers, 1968), p. 122.

pg. 17: Levering Lewis, David. *W.E.B. Du Bois Biography of a Race.* (New York, New York: Henry Holt, 1993) p. 62.

pg. 17: Mwamba, Jay. "Black History Month 2015: Grim Struggle to End the Nightmare of Lynching," *New York Daily News*, February 6, 2015. http://www.nydailynews.com/new-york/black-history-month-2015-grime-struggle-lynching-article-1.2105413.

pg. 18: Takaki, Ronald. *A Different Mirror.* (New York, NY: Back Bay Books, 1993), p. 135.

pg. 24: Levering Lewis, David. *W.E.B. Du Bois Biography of a Race.* (New York, New York: Henry Holt, 1993) p. 388.

pg. 24: *Ibid.*

CHAPTER TWO

pg. 36: Du Bois, W.E.B. "The Damnation of Women." *Darkwater: Voices From Within the Veil*. (New York, New York: Harcourt, Brace and Howe, 1920), pp. 163-164.

pg. 37: Du Bois, "The Damnation of Women," p. 164.

pg. 38: Du Bois, W. E. B. "Application to Harvard." *The Souls of Black Folk, A Norton Critical Edition*. Ed. Henry Louis Gates Jr. and Teri Hume Oliver. (New York, New York: Norton, 1999), p. 187.

pg. 41: Du Bois, W. E. B. "From A Negro Student at Harvard at the End of the Nineteenth Century." *The Souls of Black Folk, A Norton Critical Edition*. Ed. Henry Louis Gates Jr. and Teri Hume Oliver. (New York, New York: Norton, 1999), p. 188.

CHAPTER THREE

pg. 50: Washington, Booker. "The Standard Printed Version of the Atlanta Exposition Address" *The Souls of Black Folk, A Norton Critical Edition*. Ed. Henry Louis Gates Jr. and Teri Hume Oliver. (New York, New York: Norton, 1999), p. 168.

pg. 50: Washington, "The Standard Printed Version of the Atlanta Exposition Address," p. 168.

pg. 52: Du Bois, W. E. B. "Obituary of Booker T. Washington" *The Souls of Black Folk, A Norton Critical Edition*. Ed. Henry Louis Gates Jr. and Teri Hume Oliver. (New York, New York: Norton, 1999), p. 168.

CHAPTER FOUR

pg. 64: Du Bois, W. E. B. *The Souls of Black Folk, A Norton Critical Edition*. Ed. Henry Louis Gates Jr. and Teri Hume Oliver. (New York, New York: Norton, 1999), p. 10.

pg. 64: Du Bois, *The Souls of Black Folk, A Norton Critical Edition*, p. 10-11.

pg. 71: Levering Lewis, *W. E. B. Du Bois Biography of a Race*, p. 395.

CHAPTER FIVE

pg. 80: Washington, "The Standard Printed Version of the Atlanta Exposition Address," p. 168.

pg. 84: Du Bois, W. E. B. "Credo" *The Souls of Black Folk, A Norton Critical Edition*. Ed. Henry Louis Gates Jr. and Teri Hume Oliver. (New York, New York: Norton, 1999), p. 214.

pg. 85: Du Bois, W. E. B. "The Niagara Movement" *The Souls of Black Folk, A Norton Critical Edition*. Ed. Henry Louis Gates Jr. and Teri Hume Oliver. (New York, New York: Norton, 1999), p. 184.

CHAPTER SIX

pg. 103: NAACP. "Our Mission." www.naacp.org/pages/our-mission.

FURTHER INFORMATION

BOOKS

Aptheker, Herbert, ed. *Against Racism: Unpublished Essays, Papers, Addresses, 1887-1961*. W. E .B. Du Bois. Amherst, Massachusetts: University of Massachusetts Press, 1985.

Du Bois, Shirley Graham. *His Day is Marching On: Memoir of W. E. B. Du Bois*. Philadelphia, Pennsylvania: Lippincott, 1971.

Du Bois, W. E. B. *The Autobiography of W. E. B. Du Bois: A Soliloquy on Viewing My Life From the Last Decade of Its First Century*. New York: New York, International Publishers, 1968.

NAACP: Celebrating 100 Years in Pictures. Layton, Utah: Gibbs Smith, 2009.

Sullivan, Patricia. *Lift Every Voice: The NAACP and the Making of the Civil Rights Movement*. New York, New York: The New Press, 2009.

WEBSITES

March on Washington
www.history.com/topics/black-history/march-on-washington

This website features videos, an essay, and other interactive components about the famous March on Washington and civil rights protests during the 1960s.

The American Experience: The Impeachment of Andrew Johnson
www.pbs.org/wgbh/americanexperience/features/general-article/grant-impeachment

A detailed look at President Johnson's impeachment and links to other post-Civil War and Reconstruction events.

The Rise and Fall of Jim Crow: The Souls of Black Folk
www.pbs.org/wnet/jimcrow/stories_events_souls.html

A dive into Du Bois's text, along with audio recordings and PDFs of primary documents.

W. E. B. Du Bois Papers, 1803–1999 (bulk 1877–1963)
credo.library.umass.edu/view/collection/mums312

Du Bois's online archive is housed at the University of Massachusetts–Amherst and is available online here.

W. E. B. Du Bois –Rivalry with Booker T. Washington
www.biography.com/people/web-du-bois-9279924/videos/web-dubois-rivalry-with-booker-t-washington-15039555659

This site includes a video discussion about Du Bois and his relationship with Washington.

BIBLIOGRAPHY

Carr, Jane Greenway. "What a Recently Uncovered Story by W. E. B. Du Bois Tells Us About Afrofuturism." *Slate.* December 1, 2015. http://www.slate.com/blogs/future_tense/2015/12/01/_the_princess_steel_a_recently_uncovered_short_story_by_w_e_b_du_bois_and.html.

Du Bois, W. E. B. *The Autobiography of W. E. B. Du Bois: A Soliloquy on Viewing My Life from the Last Decade of Its First Century.* New York, NY: International Publishers, 1968.

Du Bois, W. E. B. *Darkwater: Voices From Within the Veil.* New York: Harcourt, Brace and Howe, 1920.

Du Bois, W. E. B. *The Souls of Black Folk.* Edited by Henry Louis Gates Jr. and Terri Hume Oliver. New York, New York: Norton, 1999.

Jackson, Harold. "The legacy of W.E.B. DuBois and the NAACP." *The Philadelphia Inquirer.* July 12, 2015. http://www.philly.com/philly/columnists/harold_jackson/20150712_The_legacy_of_W_E_B__DuBois_and_the_NAACP.html.

Lewis, David Levering. *W. E. B. Du Bois: Biography of a Race.* New York, NY: Henry Holt, 1993.

Lewis, David Levering. *W. E. B. Du Bois: The Fight for Equality and The American Century, 1919-1963*. New York, NY: Henry Holt, 2000.

Locke, Alain. Ed. *The New Negro.* New York, NY: Simon & Schuster, 1925.

"NAACP History: W.E.B. Du Bois." *NAACP.* http://www.naacp. org/pages/naacp-history-w.e.b.-dubois.

"NAACP: 100 Years of History." *NAACP.* http://www.naacp.org/ pages/naacp-history.

"Our Mission." *NAACP.* http://www.naacp.org/pages/our-mission

Takaki, Ronald. *A Different Mirror.* New York, NY: Back Bay Books, 1993.

"The March on Washington: Marking the 40th Anniversary of the Historic Civil Rights Protest." *NPR.* http://www.npr.org/news/ specials/march40th.

"W. E. B. Du Bois and the NAACP." *Virginia Historical Society.* http://www.vahistorical.org/collections-and-resources/virginia-history-explorer/civil-rights-movement-virginia/w-e-b-du-bois-and.

INDEX

Page numbers in **boldface** are illustrations. Entries in **boldface** are glossary terms.

"Of Our Spiritual Strivings", 63, 108

abolition, 11, 36, 47–49, 67, 75
accommodationist, 50
American Revolution, 9
antebellum, 47
assassination, 10
Atlanta Compromise, 18, 50, 53, 56
Atlanta University, 6–7, 18, 42–43, 59, 85, 98
Atlanta, GA, 7, 18–20, 24, 42, 44–45, 59, 71, 73, 78, 85, 94

black nationalist, 43, 59
boycott, 29, 99
Brown v. Board of Education, 28, 100, 104–105, 107
Brownies' Book, The, 92

Catholic, 14
civil rights, 7, 9, 11, 23–24, 28–29, 54, 56, 61, 70–71, 74–75, 85, 91–92, 94–95, 103, 105–106
Civil War, 5, 9, 10–11, **12–13**, 14, 18, 39, 48–49, 52, 75
Clark Atlanta University, *see* Atlanta University
Committee of Fifty, 73
Committee of Forty, 70–73
Communist, 7, 45, 59
Congregationalist , 14
Crisis, the, 7, 26, 43, 52, 54, 59, 74–75, 85, 88, **89**, 90–94, 98–99, 107–108

Darkwater: Voices from Within the Veil (autobiography), 17, 37, 95
discrimination, 7, 9, 23–24, 26, 28, 64, 66, 101–103, 106
disenfranchise, 14, 16, 28, 54, 69, 74, 106
double consciousness, 63–65, 82, 92, 108
Douglass, Frederick, **46**, 47–49, 52, 54, 64–65, 75, 79

Du Bois children,
   Burghardt Gomer, 44–45
   Nina Yolande, **44**, 45
Du Bois, Adelbert, 32–33
Du Bois, Mary (mother), 6,
   31–33, 35–37, 43
Du Bois, Nina, 19, 43–45, **44**,

Emancipation Proclamation,
   5, 8, 9, 11, 56, 69
equal rights, 5, 49, 61, 74, 83,
   95, 103

Fauset, Jessie Redmond, 45,
   59, 82, 91, **91**
feminism, 40
Fifteenth Amendment, 11,
   29, 70
Fisk Herald, The, 38–39
Fisk University, 6, 16, 37–38
Fortune, Timothy Thomas,
   34, 39, 47
Freedmen's Bureau, 10, 42

Germany, 41–42
Ghana, Africa, 7, 45
grandfather clause, 16, 99

Great Barrington, MA, 5–6,
   9, 11, 14, 17, 31–34, 36–37,
   39–40, 44, 78

Harlem Renaissance, 26, 28,
   45, 59, 81–82, 98–99, 107
Harvard University, 6, 36–38,
   40–42
Hosmer, Frank, 14, 34, 36,
Houston, Charles Hamilton,
   100, 102, 104
Hughes, Langston, 26, 91, **93**

impeach, 10
industrialist, 53

Jim Crow laws, 16–17, 49, 85
Johnson, James Weldon, 91,
   98, 108
Johnson, President Andrew, 10

King, Dr. Martin Luther, Jr.,
   23, 29
Ku Klux Klan, 100

Lincoln, President Abraham,
   10–11, 24, 69
Locke, Alain, 26, 27, 91–92

lynching, 16–17, 24–25, 56, 62, 88, 94, 100

March on Washington, 22, 23, 45, 102, 106
Marshall, Thurgood, 102, 104, **105**
migration, 25–26
multicultural education, 92

National Association for the Advancement of Colored People (NAACP), 7, 23–24, 26, 28–29, 43, 56, 58, 59, 61, 65, 69–71, 74–75, 77, 85, 88, 90, 92–95, 97–109
National Negro Committee, 56, 71, 73
National Negro Conference, 65, 69–70
New Deal, 102
New Negro, The, 26, 92
New York Globe, 34, 40, 78
Niagara Movement, 7, 43, 65–67, 67, 85, 98

Ovington, Mary, 24, 54, 55, 56, 67, 69–70, 73, 97–98

Parks, Rosa, 29
Plessy v. Ferguson, 16, 100, 102, 104
postbellum, 11
Protestants, 11

racism, 11, 24, 33–34, 39–41, 44, 63, 91
ratified, 11, 29
Reconstruction, 5, 10–11, 14, 17, 49
riot, 20, **21**, 24, 56, 67, 69, 94, 98

seceded, 11
segregation, 11, 16–19, 25–26, 28–29, 39–40, 44, 49, 56, 59, 77, 85, 88, 94, 100, 104–107
sharecropper, 25, 95
Sherman, General William T., 18
sit-in, 29
Socialist, 7, 54
Souls of Black Folk, The, 7, 58, 61–63, 62, 65, 73, 78, 80–82, 85, 88, 92, 95, 107–108
suffrage, 90

Talented Tenth, 59, 63
Thirteenth Amendment, 5, 11
two-ness, 64–65

Up from Slavery, 53, 62, 80–81

veto, 10
vigilante, 17
Villard, Oswald, 67, 69–70,
  72–73, **72**, 97–98
vocational, 36, 39, 50, 53, 80
voting, 10–11, **15**, 16–17,
  23, 29, 49, 62, 85, 90, 99,
  104–106

Walling, William, 24, 56, 65,
  67, **68**, 72–74, 97–98
Washington, Booker T., 18,
  49–54, **51**, 56, 62–63, 65–66,
  69, 73, 79–81, 83
Wells-Barnett, Ida, 56, 57, 58,
  70–71, 73, 82, **83**
white supremacy, 17, 50, 106
Wilberforce University, 42–43

ABOUT THE AUTHOR

Meghan M. Engsberg Cunningham received her BA in English and American Studies from St. Norbert College and her MA at the University of Wisconsin–Milwaukee. She completed her master's degree thesis on Charles Chesnutt's novel *The Marrow of Tradition* along with other texts that were precursors to the Harlem Renaissance. Meghan has spent time working with student writing as a writing center tutor at St. Norbert College and then as an Assistant Coordinator at the UW–Milwaukee Writing Center. She currently works in financial litigation. Meghan lives in Milwaukee with her husband, Stephen. Together they enjoy reading, running, and traveling. Her work includes *Bill "Bojangles" Robinson* in the Artists of the Harlem Renaissance series.